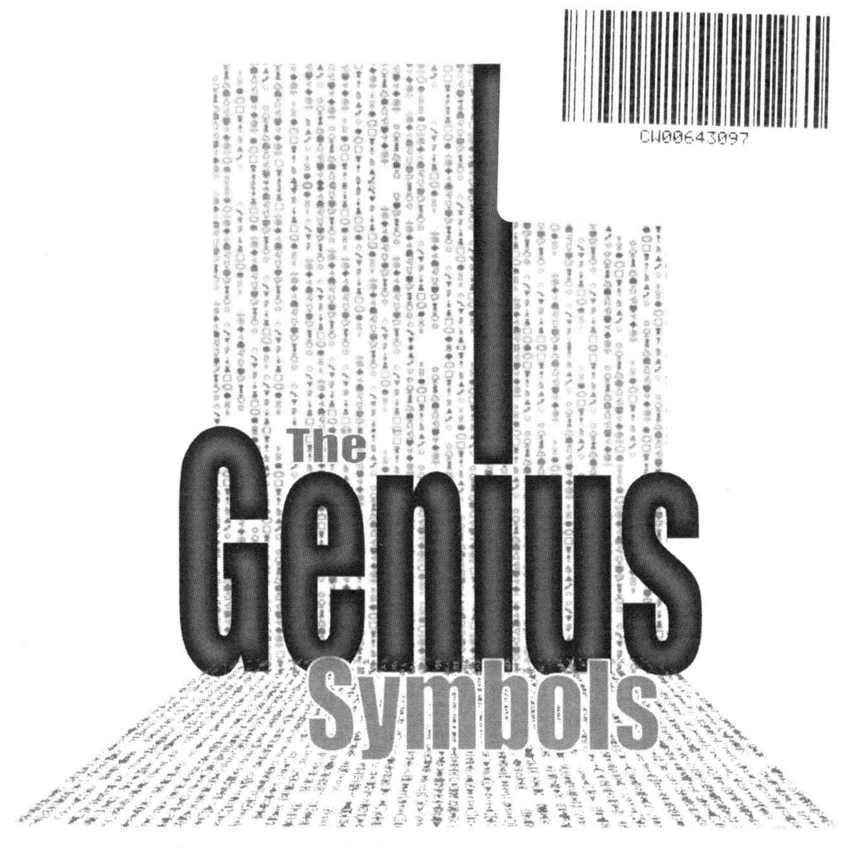

Your Portals To Creativity, Imagination & Innovation

by Dr Silvia Hartmann

Second Edition 2011

ISBN 978-1-873483-69-5

PUBLISHED BY

DragonRising Publishing

United Kingdom

The Genius Symbols:
Your Portals To Creativity, Imagination & Innovation

ISBN 978-1-873483-69-5

First Edition 2008
Second Edition 2011

Published by:

DragonRising
United Kingdom
http://DragonRising.com

Other relevant titles by this author:

Oceans Of Energy
Project Sanctuary
Events Psychology
Magic, Spells & Potions

Table of Contents

WELCOME TO YOUR GENIUS.................................. 11

Project Sanctuary 15

THE GAME IN SPACE & TIME 19

Welcome To The Greatest Human Game On Earth... 23
The Energy Mind 27
Project Sanctuary Made Easy 29
Understanding Visions 32
The Contract 34
Memories, Data Streams & Visions 37
Stepping INSIDE The Visions..................................... 40
What Can We Use Project Sanctuary For? 42

THE GENIUS SYMBOLS... 47

Co-Create A Friend With Your Energy Mind 58
It's Only Energy - Avoiding Magic Failure 62
The Threshold Shifts 63
Introducing The Genius Symbols 65
Logical Levels & The Genius Symbols 66

Space.. 71

Time 72

Weather 73

Land 74

Plant 75

Animal 76

Crystal.. 77

Angel 78

Friend... 79

People...80

Spirit...81

Aspect 82

House 83
Artefact 84
The Gift.. 85
Trade.. 86
Dragonwings.. 87
Magic.. 88
Stardust 89
Alien.. 90
Fountain 91
The Dance.. 92
Light.. 93

MAKING YOUR OWN PERSONAL GENIUS SYMBOL SET 95

Learning The Genius Symbols.. 99
Choosing Your Templates.. 101
Applying The Symbols 102

CREATING VISIONS WITH THE SYMBOLS 105

The Contract 107

GENIUS SYMBOL WARM UP EXERCISES 113

Tips On The Exercises 115
The Memory Flash Exercises 118
Pertinent Memory Exercises.. 121
The 6 Senses Exercises.. 123
Improving Your Memory With The Genius Symbols.......... 125
Ideas Exercises 126
The Gift Exercise.. 127
23 Good Ideas For Anything Exercise 129
A Very First Sanctuary.. 132
The Classic Game.. 135
Using The Symbols Inside The Game............................ 138
An Example Of The Classic Game 140

A Personalised Layout 144

Genius Symbol Patterns In Brief 145

The Classic Game 145
Single Symbol Flash Visions 146
All 23 Symbols Flash Visions 147
The Symbol Sphere 148

Genius Symbol Patterns 150

Using A Pendulum 151

GAMES TO PLAY WITH THE GENIUS SYMBOLS 153

Therapy Games 159

A Therapy Game Example 164

Healing Games 167

Past Life Regression 169
Soul Pilot 170
Meetings 171
Block Removal 172
Wishes, Wants, Needs & Desires 173
Count Your Blessings 174
The One Who Stands For Them All 175

Self Help & Personal Development 176

Adult Games 177
Law & Order Games 179
Question Games 180
Playing For A Threshold Shift 181
Playing For An Aspect 182
Relationship Games 183
Tell Your Story 185
Building A Visionary Goal 186

Creativity 190

Stories 191
"Better Stories" 194
Time Games & Time Stories 195
23 New Games 196

Creative Writing, Poetry & Paranormal Language 197
Design, Illustrations & Paintings 202
Sculpture 205
Music...207

Ideas **208**

Dealing With An Overflow Of Ideas 209
The Ideas Habitat: The Tesla Machine 213
Problem Solving 216
Inventions..218

Divination **219**

Traditional Psychic Readings & Oracles..........................219
Predictions & Psychic Phenomena.................................220
Improving Psychic Abilities...221
Remote Viewing 222
Dreams & Dream Interpretation...................................223

More Games To Exercise Your Genius **224**

"Pushing Through The Threshold" Games.....................224
The Challenge Game 226
Single Symbol Adventures..227
World Seed..228
Negative Symbols 229
Playing The Game Without A Physical Set.....................230
Into The Truly Unknown...231
Inventing Your Own Games 232

THE GENIUS SYMBOLS IN SANCTUARY 233

Visions Within Visions..235
A First Genius Symbol Game In Sanctuary 237
Playing On Behalf Of Others 238
You, The Querent 239
Living Symbol Experiences 240
Symbols & Artefacts 241

CHILDREN & THE GENIUS SYMBOLS 243

A First Symbol Experience 246
A First Story Experience 247
Giving & Receiving Gifts 248
Bedtime Stories & Meta Stories 250
Stories & Pictures 252
Little Worlds 253
Soul Piloting for Children 254
Dreams & Nightmares 255
Games for Older Children & Teenagers 256
Bringing Project Sanctuary Into The Family 258

MORE ABOUT THE GENIUS SYMBOLS 261

Symbol Meditations 263
Gift VS Trade 264
Symbol Of The Day 265
Daily Quick Meditation 266
EmoTrance Symbol Exercises 267
Using The Symbols In Daily Life 269
Blessings & Problem Help 271
The Spirit Of The Symbols 273
More Symbols, Different Symbols 275

QUESTIONS & ANSWERS 279

EPILOGUE: MORE GENIUS, PLEASE! 293

FURTHER INFORMATION 305

Books & Manuals 307
Courses 309
Audio Energy Hypnosis Programs 310
Project Sanctuary Based Books 311
Project Sanctuary Visionary Fiction by StarFields 313
SpaceNode Websites: A Genius Symbols Vision 314
Internet Resources 315

This book is dedicated
with my absolute gratitude & admiration
to all my good friends, without whom
I could not do the things I do;
to my beloved boys
who are the world to me;
and to my dear readers,
without whom it would be all be lonely, and pointless.

Brightest blessings and starfalls of delights,

Silvia

Welcome To YOUR Genius...

Much has been talked and written about how we might get to a point where people's inherent genius can begin to come to the fore and manifest itself FOR REAL in a person's life.

I have worked on this for about five decades years now and, based on my personal experiences and those of the people who have used my strategies and helped me test my ideas and techniques, I would say that we have a sound theory which powers a set of strategies to do exactly that - get a person, ANY PERSON who sincerely wants to, to contact their "genius within" and create their own genius solutions to their problems and contributions.

I am very lucky that during the time of my research computers arose and proved once and for all that to be able to crunch numbers fast and furiously or to store masses of data that can be regurgitated at the push of a button IS NOT GENIUS.

Genius is a higher form of solution; something that is so cohesive and in many ways, so "out of the ordinary", that a computer could never have thought of it.

The classic example that is used in our times is that of Einstein who got his ideas for the many formulae he ended up composing by having a vision of himself riding on a beam of light.

Another story that is often told is that of the scientist who had a vision of a spiral staircase and thus figured out how DNA hangs together.

In the past it was often so that mastery in mechanical execution - be it in maths, putting words together, applying paint to a canvas or in any other modality such as playing the piano, or welding metal - was confused with genius.

It is quite a simple distinction though and our computers today have taught us this well and truly.

Hundreds, thousands of people can learn the techniques to paint the Mona Lisa.

Hundreds of thousands can learn to play the Adagio in G Minor flawlessly.

You can teach people, even though it may take a long time, to re-write Einstein's maths and physics symbols.

But the original IDEA that sits behind these things is what is genius.

The genius is in the original vision, not in the eventual execution.

- **To be a genius, you need to have visions.**

I have developed and modelled a method to make this genius accessible, and it is actually surprisingly easy - if you know how.

There is a place within our systems where this genius lives.

All we have to do is to go there, and to learn how to communicate with it.

Amazingly and wonderfully, you can not do that by being "smart" or "clever".

You can only do it by being honest.

This simple fact amuses me highly on many different levels and I could say much about the inherent beauty and justice of this; but we are here today to find out about the Genius Symbols, a really simple form of alphabet that will allow you to start communicating with the source of human genius which all of us possess by right of birth, to learn how this genius thinks and expresses itself; and to use these genius systems to find resolutions for your problems that will blow you away - even if you're only a beginner.

Project Sanctuary

There is a mind space to which the human conscious can and does travel on a regular basis; a place in space and time that is quite real and simply a structural part of the human systems.

I call this space Project Sanctuary.

This is the domain of what I call the energy mind, and which others in the past have called the unconscious or subconscious mind, neither of which is either accurate or helpful in our dealings with this form of human awareness.

The energy mind is a part of the energy body just as the brain is a part of the physical body; a system that really exists and that "does its thing".

The thing it does seems like magic to the conscious mind and sometimes, it frightens the conscious mind that doesn't understand how to think like that.

So I have devised a safe meeting platform, a place in space and time located at the crossroads and on the border where the conscious mind and the energy mind touch each other, where we can go in consciousness in order to start learning about the mysterious system of the human totality that is the energy mind.

We call this place at the crossroads **Project** Sanctuary because it is an ongoing project of exploration.

The symbols you will find in this manual were co-created between the conscious mind and the energy mind to help this exploration along and to become easy access portals that will make it much easier for you to hold your focus, direct your attention and to begin to stream information from the energy mind.

You will be surprised how easy this is to do once you've got the hang of the basics; but as I always say, we are simply using what the Creator gave us in the first place and what we were MEANT TO USE all along, so of course, it would be easy.

When a person has been strapped to a chair all day, every day, from the moment they were born, and they only got to move their legs at night, and finally they're asked for the first time to stand up or even to walk, of course you're going to get some disturbances.

The person might be convinced that they don't even have legs at all, or that their legs don't work properly; they might not know how to use them to walk or stand or even rise into a standing position.

But after a little practise, some feeling and movement will come back, especially if that person has a positive attitude to the process and a true motivation to really rise, walk once more, to run even, and to dance!

That's a pretty good analogy for bringing our energy minds back on track and back into our daily lives from which they were banished in the dark ages way back when; it's just a matter of a bit of practise, and to figure out how these systems we were all born with actually work, what they feel like - and what they can do for you.

Project Sanctuary makes this process of re-discovery easy and exciting; and the Project Sanctuary "Genius Symbols" make it even easier - so easy in fact that a child can do this without any problems whatsoever.

We are going to visit, create and explore cohesive "worlds", habitats as we call them, which work in context and are incredibly information dense – just like the real world.

We are going to learn to not be consciously overwhelmed by this information density which is the hallmark of how the energy mind stores and processes information, but to relax and learn to step into the flow of this information, go with the flow of this information, and to begin to interact in this information flow.

- **This information flow is our visions.**

We are going to proceed on a trial and error base, guided by direct and instantaneous feedback, and we are going to learn what works, and what doesn't.

We are going to begin to understand the ways of the energy mind, and as we do, our intelligence begins to increase exponentially; our abilities to compute multi-level dynamic systems will increase exponentially; and our ideas of what and who we are and what we can achieve in this life will begin to change in step with that.

A true genius isn't a bumbling idiot who had one single good idea in their entire lives.

A true genius is someone who can tap into the flow of their own energy mind at will and USE THIS to create something new, something of value, something that is a contribution to the evolution of man.

You can be that true genius if you want to be, and it isn't even difficult.

All you have to do is to take a deep breath, let go of all that jumble of ideas and conscious thoughts that never get any person anywhere, let go of all these ideas that intelligence or genius are hard work, difficult or take a long time, or are painful in some way, and instead of that, begin to think yourself towards a place where <u>being a genius is what is being human is all about</u> in the first place, towards a place where true learning and information are light, easy and delightful, and a time when that has become an absolute reality for us all.

So let us now begin at the beginning...

The Game In Space & Time

Let's play a game!
A game in space and time,
a game of mind and thought,
of energy, attention –
but before we start
to step a way from every day,
I must explain
the nature of this game,
for this is not
a competition or a sport of war,
instead, it is a dance of exploration
of worlds within, the
worlds without restriction,
without hesitation, without limitations -

It is a game a child could play
so that we might discover more
about the wondrous universe
and how it does respond
to the lightest touch,
the brightest, newest thought,
and how it looks, and tastes and sounds and feels
so good and right when we discover...

Star velvet,
filled with living light,
the realms of all creation -
infinite potential,
at your beck and call –
all ready now for you,
your universal sandbox
is awaiting you...

Welcome To The Greatest Human Game On Earth...

The one true game In Space and Time.

We call it Project Sanctuary, for it has to have a name - all things do.

And for a moment, let us think what Sanctuary means.

It means a safe place, a protected place, a place where you will find respite, and safe keeping, but more than that.

The Sanctuary is beautiful.

It resonates with life.

It is filled with magic, holiness and it dances - this is not a sad place.

Loneliness doesn't live here.

Heartache melts away.

Anger, rage, cannot survive the joy and beauty that is so infused in everything, that radiates from everything and through everything, becomes a part of you.

There is no chaos here, no confusion, no ugliness – just a total perfection of beauty, clarity, logic so profound, it breaches into holiness without even trying.

The Sanctuary is filled with song, and it is infinite - it stretches, reaches through all and every plane and level of existence, it is here and now, and long ago, and will be till the end of time and then beyond - and then beyond again.

The Sanctuary belongs to humans by all right of birth; we can go there, and it always is awaiting us, was awaiting us, and those of us who walked there, we brought back the works of art, the music and the wonderful ideas that are still celebrated by humanity for being so inspired, different from the ordinary, magical, a gift from the Gods.

So it is indeed.

The Sanctuary is a gift of the Creative Order; it is a way for us to travel where we will, to live as we will, to experience things that we cannot experience in our fleshly bodies, and still, we can experience and learn.

It is a fantastic gift.

It makes being a human being worthwhile.

Sanctuary is the antidote to being afraid of death because you've recognised it, thought about it, which is so unlike our animal friends and companions in these incarnations would experience.

They don't know of future or past and they just live; we on the other hand can live not just in the now, but also in the past and in the future, and often we do live in alternate realities that we mistake for how it really is!

Some call the realms of Sanctuary the realms of consciousness in energy; and that is fine, and I don't mind, but the truth is that thinking ABOUT it hasn't ever made a single man grow wise; and what we do not know, we certainly can talk about for all eternity and never get a resolution, or anything other than possibly laryngitis for our troubles.

➢ **You cannot understand Sanctuary by analysing it.**

It's too complex for that.

Not too *complicated*, please understand - complications are what the conscious mind brings to the party.

The natural world is simply infinitely complex, and yet we all understand it innately, we were made for it, and it for us, and we belong together.

To know what a ripe orange tastes like, it doesn't do to read books about it, to talk to others who have no idea as well and try and guess; and looking at the pictures and the paintings that were drawn, the songs that were sung or the sculptures made in honour of that fabulous experience will never tell you how an orange really tastes. How it feels in your hand, how it smells, and what happens in your mouth and radiating through into your whole existence when you take a bite...

Now, you really know.

You have experienced it.

Now, you can write a song, or tell a story, draw a picture, even make a diagram, a symbol that encompasses for you that whole experience of eating your first ever orange.

You could make a song.

And you could dance it too; design an outfit to remind you or perhaps a magic charm that helps to carry what it was.

➢ **There is NO OTHER WAY to learn but just to play.**

And there is nothing more exciting than to play in Sanctuary.

There are stories there that will change your mind, and some will bring about a change of heart, and even change your life.

There are experiences that will teach you about so many things that you could otherwise have NEVER known, or touched, or interacted with.

There are colours and sounds, scents and tastes, feelings and sensations, visions, dreams, amazing, so amazing each and every one, and all those things are richly felt, and deeply held, and they are true and magical the same.

Playing in Sanctuary is truly, the Greatest Human Game On Earth.

ALL other games that people play come from Sanctuary.

ALL stories, movies, novels, poems, books and even what you see on the TV comes from Sanctuary.

ALL language, symbols, measures, artefacts and science, it all comes from and through Sanctuary.

All innovation and invention, all new ideas, all RIGHT ideas, it all comes from Sanctuary and nowhere else.

And finally, all religious insights, all enlightenment experiences, all visions and all dreams that make the base for what the people of the earth might worship from one millennium to the next, all that comes from and through Sanctuary as well.

Are you impressed yet?

Possibly a little overwhelmed?

No need to be.

We were DESIGNED for this!

And now the time has come that we can start to play...

Please meet our dance partner…

The Energy Mind

Unlike the older approaches where messages from the energy mind were downloaded into the conscious mind and then carried away for conscious analysis after the fact, we do something deeply different when we play Project Sanctuary - we go to the place where the visions are happening.

The conscious mind steps across the divide, much as you would in a lucid dream, and we step into the visions and interact with them in real time.

As you can imagine, this has too many advantages over the old way of trying to decipher a message in a bottle, drawn in a foreign language, out of context, out of time and place, using what we know of THIS world as a guide, to even start listing them all.

- **Conscious minds cannot "analyse" visions any more than they can create them.**

The Sanctuary realms are infinite, multi-level, multi-layered, multi-dimensional, totally interactive and entirely FLUID by nature; they know no gravity other than what we might bring to them, and time and space is LIQUID there.

When we go there, and when we act there, we learn wonderful things, amazing things, and many of those are just exactly what the doctor ordered to put our lives "down here in the hard" back on track, back into perspective, make them work so much more smoothly and CORRECTLY at that.

But the true purpose of playing Project Sanctuary is the game, in and of itself. For sure, we get benefits, threshold shifts, new ideas and all manner of wondrous gifts of creativity, insight, learning and experience, but that is just the icing on the cake.

That's not why we play Sanctuary.

We play Sanctuary because we can, and because I believe WE MUST, because if we don't, we're missing the point of what being a human being is all about!

Now it is true that to the uninitiated, the Sanctuary realms can be very strange. But that's OK, because we have a very, very close relative of ours who lives there all the time, and who knows EVERYTHING about those planes of existence that a human could ever know - and that is our energy mind.

- **Our energy mind sends us data streams of energy.**

If we receive them into consciousness in a flash, that's a vision; if we then step into that data stream, we are INSIDE THE VISION and we have entered structurally into a communication with the energy mind.

When that happens, magic really begins to reign.

It is EXTRAORDINARY how the act of visiting with the energy mind and experiencing those data streams in a very personal, first person basis enriches us - as people, individually, and our lives.

As we play the games of Project Sanctuary, we learn more and more about these realms, how to make changes there, how to ask for help and advice, and so many other things besides, you simply can't list them all.

Playing Project Sanctuary is truly life changing, and it is absolutely, The Greatest Human Game On Earth.

Project Sanctuary Made Easy

I have played in Sanctuary for many years, and never really given much thought to how I could make it easier for others to step into this. It seemed easy enough already - ask for a time of day, ask for a location, some vegetation, a landscape, a friend or two, a dwelling, and the energy mind will provide the answers, direct our conscious attention to the right place in the data stream, and off we go!

And it **is** easy enough - and therein lies a part of the problem.

It is so easy and the myriads of available data streams are SO TOTALLY INFINITE, that the conscious mind gets boggled by it all and doesn't know what to do next.

It's like standing in front of a buffet with every fruit from not just this galaxy, not just all galaxies, and not just all alternate galaxies in all possible alternate dimensions, but all that have ever been, and all those still to come, on display for you to choose from.

How do you choose from that?

The conscious mind is the one who has to make the choice, takes the first steps **into** Sanctuary. Without that, nothing else can happen.

So I thought of a way to make it easier for people, something to hold on to, something simple yet wide open to help people retain their focus.

Over a period of two months, my energy mind and my conscious mind tried and tested many symbols, until they came together and agreed on the 23 Genius Symbols you find in this book.

The truly revolutionary quality of the Genius Symbols comes from exactly that communication process – these are not conscious symbols, and neither are they "just channelled" without reservation.

The Genius Symbols arose IN CONSULTATION between the two minds and represent an agreement, a shared symbol set that serves as a kind of Rosetta Stone so we can finally begin to transmit information DIRECTLY back and forth between the energy mind, and the conscious mind.

It is truly extraordinary how this consultation, this communication has produced a set of symbols that are readily recognised by BOTH aspects of the human thought process; that is at the core why they are so easy to use, and so immensely simple yet so immensely deep and rich, all at the same time.

As I began to use the symbols to start further communications, I began to understand that for the first time, here was also a DIRECT WAY to steer the entire process of communicating and CONSULTING with the energy mind.

The conscious mind starts the game by stating a desired outcome, very precisely indeed using the Art Solutions contracts; the energy mind responds by giving its unique view of the solution in the forms of visions we call stories.

This is where it all ended for the oracles of old; but when you work with Project Sanctuary and the Genius Symbols, this is not the end at all.

Instead of now being stuck with trying to figure out some cryptic metaphorical message, we consciously get to ask questions, find further elucidation, and even **change** the vision – indeed, we continue the game, this consultation, until a breakthrough occurs. This breakthrough is a moment of understanding, a "Eureka!" moment that is felt in the body like a lightning strike, and we call it **a threshold shift.**

That is truly unprecedented as a concept or technique and the results are simply stunning, as you will find out for yourself.

With the conscious mind being a full playing partner, a dance partner in its own right, neither a slave or a master to the energy mind but instead a peer based intelligence system that is in fact **structurally required** to make the insights and inspirations of the energy mind work in the hard, we are in a totally different, brand new paradigm of human visioning altogether.

Now, in amidst all that infinity of choice, we get to pick the one fruit from that multiverse buffet that will help us the most with this one exact headache we have right here, right now.

Now we know, now we look - and look! There's one fruit that seems to be glowing, we are drawn to it, it feels so right - that must be the right one!

Of course, it is because our energy mind has now understood the request and acted in return to demonstrate to us clearly which one of these many choices is required for this particular purpose.

But then, the conscious mind steps forward as we decide to take that fruit and eat it – and it is only then that the game is complete, and a threshold shift has been reached, and the full potential of the two human systems of mind and thought working in harmony finally becomes revealed.

And that is **visionary genius in action**.

Understanding Visions

When we get a flash of a vision, let's say my example of the alien fruit buffet from all of time and space and the multifold dimensions, that's one thing.

That is more than enough to paint a picture, or to hold it there and tune into it to write a song, make a sculpture and so forth.

Stepping **into** the vision in consciousness is another story altogether, and here we have the **Project Sanctuary STORY** - the flow of events that defines our interaction with the Sanctuary realm.

- **We interact with the data stream through stories**.

Please understand that nothing exists in a vacuum.

All things are connected, all are interrelated.

There can be - in terms of the energy mind! - no buffet of alien fruit simply floating in space.

It doesn't work.

There has to be a context, a table, gravity to stop the fruit from flying up into the air.

The table has to stand on a surface, and there has to be a planet. This whole thing **has to be somewhere and somewhen.**

The entire context is integral to the whole story.

You could tell it like this, "Once upon a time in a galaxy far away, there was this planet, and on this planet there was this palace, and in the largest room of the palace there stood many tables, and on those tables you could find fruit from everywhere, and everywhen..."

Everything in Project Sanctuary has a story, and everything IS a story - data, energetic information, energy that flows from one thing to the next, from one moment to the next.

True reality is always unfolding, always evolving.

When we step into the story or vision, we are stepping into an unfolding river of events. We are inside of this river of events, and being there, we are adding to those events - and we may change them, too.

- **Stories and visions from your energy mind are translations of the data stream into shapes and forms and occurrences we can consciously understand.**

A purple double cascading semi-inverted blob doesn't make any sense to us and there's nothing we can do with that, or about that (at least not to start with, or until we have learned how to understand much more abstract visions and communications!), but if we were to look at a fountain that got clogged up instead, we would understand all sorts about the situation - there is a problem with flow, there is a clog, we can solve this problem.

- **Project Sanctuary stories and visions are energy streams.**

It's important to remember that before we start out, and then it's important to forget it as we become a part of the story, of the vision, of the energy events and either learn and listen, or actively begin to change the stories.

This is very, very easy - it is natural to people to understand and to do, even very small and unfinished people we call children have no problem at all with stepping into a story, interacting with the story, changing it if necessary.

And the Project Sanctuary Genius Symbols solve the problem as to which story we should choose to start interacting with the amazing Sanctuary realms.

Here, we get to choose a topic we want to play for, and play with.

The Contract

Before we start to unfold a vision and a story using the Genius Symbols, we - our conscious selves - create an agreement or contract with the energy mind as to how it can help us on this occasion.

- **We tell the energy mind what we want in the clearest and most direct terms.**

The contract is a statement that contains the information the energy mind needs in order to respond with the correct vision or story; and in turn, we undertake to listen and to learn, and if we need to, to act on behalf of all of us to bring about changes for the better.

This is the contract we enter into with our dance partner, the energy mind, and it makes it very easy to get started with the greatest game on Earth - <u>because it is always highly relevant to ourselves.</u>

When we play on behalf of another person, or a group of other persons, we can discuss the contract before we take it to the energy mind to make sure it is as precise and as open as possible.

We can ask the energy mind **anything**.

We can ask it to assist us in **anything**.

The energy mind will answer us reliably every time because that is how it works, and what it does, what it is supposed to do.

When the energy mind has answered, we can then consciously enter into a two way communication with the events of the story or vision, and that is where the magic and excitement really begins to unfold.

How exactly the agreement is phrased is up to each individual. A simple example would be a form such as this:

"Dear energy mind, give me something today that will resolve my problems with my ex-husband, once and for all."

"Dear energy mind, give me the perfect vision for this person, to be the best gift I can give to them today."

"Dear energy mind, I need something for my new project to make it work..."

"Dear energy mind, give me the perfect vision for the new advertising client..."

"Dear energy mind, give me something to resolve my problems with time."

"Dear energy mind, give a story for my five year old so he won't be bullied any more at school."

"Dear energy mind, show me the error in the presuppositions of this theory so I can make it work."

"Dear energy mind, give me something to feel better, and to heal me, and to make my future brighter, and to give me life and hope."

In the last example please notice there were a lot of **and**s.

The energy mind is an amazing system, and it can come up with the most amazing solutions – even when multiple components are involved and the computations become so complex that the conscious mind would simply give up trying to work out a solution that could possibly encompass them all, **and resolve them all.**

The energy mind itself has such extraordinary capacities for computing super-complex realities that is already astonishing; in potential, there is even the further possibility that what it doesn't know, it can go somewhere to get help with that, from other and also higher sources.

You can put as many **and**s into your contract as you like.

> *"Dear energy mind, give me something today that will make me happy* ***and*** *help me stay married* ***and*** *give me more freedom* ***and*** *joy* ***and*** *money* ***and*** *respect* ***and*** *purpose in life."*

Even direct conflicts can be addressed like that, or problems and issues that you have which seem to be impossible to get on the same page or find a solution that would satisfy all parties.

If you are playing with a group, your agreement can be:

> *"Give me the perfect story today that will help everyone,* ***and*** *bring this group closer together,* ***and*** *make them have the time of their lives and teach me something important too!"*

But that's only the tip of the iceberg.

With a little experience, you can make your agreements as specific and as global as you want them to be, as basic and mundane and as highly spiritual and esoteric as you need at the time.

It is true that for the energy mind, "no job's too small" - and there are definitely no jobs that are too large, or it can't handle.

In the games section, there will be lots of different examples to give you many ideas on how to get playing, and gain important experience in dancing with your own energy mind.

Memories, Data Streams & Visions

We have noted that visions are data streams from the energy mind. But what of memories?

Well, memories are also stored in the form of energetic data in our systems - and that is the only place where any "events" of the past still exist, and the only form they still exist in.

As soon as anything has happened and has been experienced, it turns from a "real event" into a memory, or as we would say, it becomes data.

As soon as that happens, we are no longer dealing with any kind of external reality, but only with the data that exists inside one person - intrapersonal reality, in other words.

Structurally, there is no difference between a vividly experienced memory, a dream, or a vision. All these manifestations are only data streams from the energy mind.

Memories being data, and only data now - we call this, "It's only energy!" - can be used and dealt with exactly the same as one would deal with any other type of data.

Which means that you can read your data only, or do that thing we do and step inside the data stream in order to change it.

This sometimes happened accidentally in the past, without people knowing what they were doing, and this "stepping inside the data stream and thereby changing it forever" caused what was called False Memories. False memories confused the living daylights out of therapists, psychologists and those to whom this had happened by accident.

This is very different from deliberately and consciously working with the data of memories, in order to learn from them, or in some cases, to interact with them, to change them. Here, we are talking not of "False Memories" but of changed memories and we know what we are doing and why, and of course, we even retain the memory of having changed a memory in the first place.

Memory data is an important part of communicating with the energy mind.

The energy mind uses memory data to try and communicate with us, sending us “memory visions” to warn us, or let us know that there is a problem with a system that needs attention.

For example, every person has the experience of “suddenly remembering something.” We call this “receiving a data stream from the energy mind” because that is what it is; but mostly, such communication attempts by the conscious mind are misunderstood, not welcomed, and not acted upon, which makes the conscious/energy mind divide grow wider as time goes on.

Memories are very important data streams.

We know much more, and have experienced much more, than we give ourselves credit for. We have accumulated a huge amount of “wisdom learning” which is when you learn something through experience, and it becomes a part of you in a much more structural way than something you might have read about in a book, but not experienced in your own body and as result of your own thoughts and actions.

All this wisdom is stored in a person's matrix, all the experiences of a lifetime, all the thoughts, deeds, feelings, sensations, sights, sounds, tastes, smells and emotions.

That is a huge amount of precious data that the energy mind can use to communicate with us in a very personal way; and by treating memories exactly like you would any other type of data from the energy mind, as though each memory is in fact a habitat that you can enter into consciously, learn more, interact with, change and be changed in doing so is an incredibly powerful and freeing way of working with our own minds.

We can create contracts with the energy mind to show us relevant memory data as well as creating fluid new data.

This does something quite remarkable.

Instead of having to think in terms of endless "new" ideas, we are not just confined to new ideas, but we have all possible ideas at our mental fingertips.

We can ask for "the right idea" - and this may not be some revolutionary new insight that has never been before, but an application of an existing piece of knowledge or wisdom that has been overlooked instead.

We will see many examples of using The Genius Symbols to work with memories as visions and as habitats that we can step into as we go along; for now, I would just like you to note how powerful it is to have access to not just endless streams of creativity that are new and custom made for you, but also, to all and everything you have ever learned about how the world works, and much besides.

This is achieved by treating all energy mind generated data and including our memories as something we can take charge of, that we can understand, that we can step into the data stream and interact with it directly, and at will.

Stepping INSIDE The Visions

The purpose of Project Sanctuary is to visit a stable world or a habitat in which events take place that you don't "make up yourself" by consciously thinking about it, but which are shown to you by your energy mind (previously known as the unconscious or subconscious mind) instead.

When we have found such a world, or a habitat, we can literally step into it, step INSIDE THE VISION.

We consciously get to interact with what happens there – we can explore, see things, hear things, feel things. We can touch and move objects, fly around, take up many different viewpoints, talk with all manner of creatures, make love, discover treasure, resolve problems, ask questions, undertake adventures, find healing, mystery and fun in truly infinitely different and surprising ways.

Unlike a daydream or a general fantasy that is flighty, here one moment and gone the next, PS habitats are very stable and you can go there again and again. The greatest fun, however, is that although the Project Sanctuary worlds are very stable, they also evolve all by themselves – they are very real indeed.

This is what makes Project Sanctuary endlessly exciting. You get to experience events, and stories, and instead of being a bystander, you are a player in the unfolding game of which you don't know the outcome yet – at least not until you have finished the game.

Project Sanctuary is full of surprises. What surprises people the most is how easy and natural it is to enter into the game, and how their energy mind begins to respond with visions and feelings, solutions, and events that you "would have never thought of in a million years!"

Only – you DID think of it, it really was YOU. It just wasn't the you normally think of when you think of yourself – what gave you the visions, the solutions and these exciting adventures was **a part of you** that most people only get to meet in dreams or in the rarest unpredictable moments of creativity.

Everyone has an energy mind, and everyone can learn to actually use it.

The Project Sanctuary Genius Symbols are going to make it easy for you to establish a kind of alphabet that will help you communicate successfully with your own energy mind any time you want, and get its help, advice, visions and wisdom for real practical use and positive changes in your life.

What Can We Use Project Sanctuary For?

What exactly you want to use Project Sanctuary for is entirely up to you.

A lot of people use it for some form of therapy – to rescue child aspects that were mistreated or sad and lonely, unloved and uncared for, for example; to resolve relationships with mother, father, perpetrators etc.; to overcome bereavement; to work with the events memories of their lives and change or evolve them, and find true personal healing on many different levels.

Many people use Project Sanctuary for healing. There is rest and relaxation to be had in incredibly beautiful worlds that are custom made by you for you – healing fountains, fabulous sleep and dream habitats, wonderful nature energies, magic potions and meeting angels and wise healers are amongst the many different ways in which we can learn to support, nourish and heal ourselves in Sanctuary.

Another favourite for many is spiritual and personal development.

Project Sanctuary is essentially a universal sandbox for us children of the Universe, to play in safety, to have a protected platform where we can meet and converse with, learn from higher powers, angels, prophets and especially, make contact with our own higher aspects. Project Sanctuary is entirely structural so it doesn't conflict with any form of religion; it is entirely up to the individual person whether they choose to meet in their own beautiful garden, or a temple, or any landscape of their choice with Jesus, or Mohammed, or Krishna, or Buddha or Gaia. Making a direct and personal connection with their own saints and deities is a wonderful experience for people.

Many people turn to Project Sanctuary because of its intelligence enhancing effects. Working WITH the energy mind allows us consciously to understand many things much better, become more flexible in the usage of our intelligence, and to be able to deal with much, MUCH more systemic complexity without becoming consciously overwhelmed or needing to reduce reality to a point where the oversimplified models become structurally impoverished and practically useless.

Linguists and logicians appreciate Project Sanctuary because it teaches the structure of translating energy data into language and unlocks the "worlds behind the symbols of man" in a personal and perfect way.

Many people use Project Sanctuary as a Tesla machine, to create habitats specifically for the purpose of trying out all manner of systems and techniques in speed and safety, to bring the results back into the hard and know that they will work there.

For some, the autogenic aspects of Project Sanctuary experiences are the most attractive usage of this space. With just a little experience and motivation, physical experiences in Sanctuary bridge across the divide and become physical reality; this is useful for sports, fitness, weight loss, sex, health and all manner of physically based activities and experiences.

Others use Project Sanctuary because of its incredible ability to make all forms of creativity flower. Project Sanctuary generates AT WILL literally endless materials for totally original and truly amazing paintings, stories, poems, songs, works of art of all kinds. Project Sanctuary very literally takes creativity and makes it not just available to all, but also amazingly reliable.

Of course, Project Sanctuary is a first choice for those who want to enhance or discover their psychic skills and talents, develop their psychic circuitry, reclaim lost resources of clairvoyance and clairaudience, contact the spirit world, experience true lucid awareness, out of body travel and much besides.

Finally, there are many people who just appreciate Project Sanctuary for the wonderful opportunities to relax, play, enjoy and simply have a wonderful time, interacting autogenically with fabulous environments, luxurious experiences and of course, all manner of people and other beings in very real sense.

Playing Project Sanctuary makes all the most advanced forms of human mind movements natural and easy. For example, autogenic experiences, lucid awareness states and really intense full-body sensations develop naturally and simply as you play the games you are drawn to the most. Guided by your own fascinations and what you love to do best, between you and your energy mind this extraordinary and totally personalised "practice and learning program" comes into being that keeps you fascinated every step of the way.

It is a fact that being able to play Project Sanctuary adds a new dimension to a person's life.

- **Being able to play Project Sanctuary well gives a person a set of skills and resources unlike any other that go with them wherever they are, and whatever their external or material circumstances might be.**

Love, beauty, adventure, excitement, sex, healing, creativity, magic and spirituality are then only a thought away, always at the ready, always there as a wellspring of the most amazing resources – and this wellspring does not come from a guru, or from high above, but it is the birthright of every living person, it comes from inside themselves.

No-one can take this away from you. Once you can play Sanctuary, you will never not know what to do next, ever again. The world will open up and become endlessly exciting again, and you will learn to see, know, hear and feel so much more, understand so much more, it is truly a wonderful gift.

This is a gift that will keep on giving, even when your skin has long turned wrinkly, your eyes can't see clearly any more and your legs can't walk any longer.

But what is most exciting of all is the experience of using our minds FINALLY the way they were designed to be used – **the conscious mind working together with the energy mind, to SERVE YOU, to PROTECT YOU, to INSPIRE you, and to get you your highest outcomes and the greatest joy possible, right here, in this life.**

Once you have entered into Sanctuary, the world will never be sad or grey again – at least not for any length of time.

That is the reality of Project Sanctuary.

For more detailed information, please see the Project Sanctuary manual; this workbook is designed especially **to get you to play** – by yourself, with your children, with other people.

- **Please know that all the many benefits of Project Sanctuary cannot be gained by "thinking about" what it is and how it works – you will only get the benefits by PLAYING THE GAME.**

Every single time you play "The Game In Space & Time" we call Project Sanctuary, you learn, you expand, you heal, and you become more intelligent.

The more you play, the greater the benefits become.

I hope sincerely that the Genius Symbols and the games you find in this book will help you to play more, try many different games, and different kinds of games.

This is truly, the greatest human game on Earth.

And that is so because it is **your game**.

The Genius Symbols

A Project Sanctuary experience is a vision which we enter into and we can choose to change, if we need to.

Instead of having random visions or memories exploding into our minds, we travel in consciousness to the time and space where the events of the vision take place – we enter into the energy stream, into the story.

Every story has a stage, a place and time where this story or these events are happening, and we call this stage **a habitat.**

When we go to have a Project Sanctuary experience, our consciousness travels to the habitat and steps into it – and it really is as easy as that.

The simplest and most direct way to find your Project Sanctuary habitat, or the special world with all its events, structures, beings, plants, landscapes and adventures, **the only one that is just the right one FOR YOU, AT THIS TIME**, is to ask the energy mind some clearly defined and specific questions.

- **Consciously, we cannot know the answers to this.**

It is the energy mind who has to supply answers to these questions, take us to the right place and time in the data stream, that is what produces the visions, the sensations, the colours, the sounds, the scents, the tastes, the feelings – and the story.

We discover a habitat in time and space by finding out about its unique space and time coordinates - that is how we find our way to a real habitat as opposed to a pointless hallucination, **a real place** in the endless worlds of energy streams and rivers which we can enter into with our consciousness.

We start with the contract so that the energy mind knows what we are looking for, for example by saying that we want to find a habitat right now that is the perfect habitat to introduce you to Project Sanctuary.

A place and a time of rest, of peace, of healing, of support and of living excitement and joy – **the perfect sanctuary for you**, right now.

We ask:

What is the time of day?

Dawn, Morning, Midday, Afternoon, Evening, Dusk, Night?

What is the time of year?

Spring, Summer, Autumn or Winter?

Choose one answer from each of the two sets of choices. You can choose it at random if you will; there is no such thing as "random". Somehow, you know which one is right for you, right here and now, at this time, in this space.

If you pay attention to your body sensations, or if you are familiar with EmoTrance, you will feel a yes/no response to each one and it will be unarguable to you which one is the right one.

- **These body sensations are direct feedback mechanisms from the energy body - and thereby, from the energy mind.**

So even if you can't see or hear an answer as yet, you can certainly feel which one is the right one, and that's all you need to worry about right now.

Now we have our time of day and the time of year established, we add more information to our developing "perfect place in time and space."

The next question we ask is:

What is the weather?

On this day, at this time of day, is it sunny? Rainy? Windy? Warm? Cold? Dry? Moist? This information will come from "somewhere" and this somewhere is a communication from your energy mind.

Accept whatever comes to you without prejudice, add this information to the time of day and season of the year you already have.

Remember that you don't have to see anything yet, but do pay attention to your body feelings. Your body knows exactly what a wind still day in late November feels like, or a moment just before a storm in summer, or a sunny day in early spring and so forth.

The conscious mind can easily go off on a wild goose chase and *think* of all those things, but it is your FEELINGS that will guide you in the worlds of energy for now and until you have become accustomed to knowing the difference between a mere fancy, and a true energy mind vision where you are indeed connected to the data stream itself.

Now we have a time, and we have the weather.

The next question we ask is:

What is the landscape?

Most people "see" something – colours perhaps to start with, like the misty green greys of a rainforest, the yellows of a desert, the greys of a mountain range.

Others feel it first – they might notice they are standing in soft grass, or on wet sand, or dried earth and that is what provides the information.

Sometimes people hear the birdsong first, or the squawking of seagulls that tells them they are on the shores of an ocean.

Remember that the information from the energy mind comes in the form of streams of energy data which have to be translated into movies, pictures, feelings, sounds and visions.

It is only then that the conscious mind gets the content of the data stream and we can consciously recognise the data stream and say, "Oh yes, it's a forest road..."[1]

---

[1] In the past, people thought that unless your "visual" internal representation system was extraordinary, you couldn't possibly have "visions". This is of course erroneous as the data stream gives you full body visual, hyper visual, auditory, gustatory, olfactory, and most especially, kinaesthetic (feeling) information ALL AT THE SAME TIME just as it would be if you were walking down a road. For Project Sanctuary stories, all representations come online together eventually; people differ in which representation system they prefer to enter the story with.

We may now refine the habitat further and ask about...

the plants and vegetation,

if there are any animals noticeable,

...and in the case of a first Sanctuary, we would also ask for a dwelling. This is a house, a man-made object, the first man-made object on this plane where all so far has been natural.

We call it a dwelling rather than a house because we don't want to prejudice what it is too much – some people might have a tent, or a log cabin, or a hut, or a very exquisite castle, or even a habitable cave.

With the dwelling in place, the first habitat is now ready for you, complete and actual.

- **Now, we step into it and move around, get to know this habitat.**

To begin with, this often happens in flashes of this and that; the data stream isn't smoothly translated yet and we tune in and out at the beginning.

Just keep asking questions and speaking out aloud, describing things to yourself or another who will listen as you move around the habitat and begin to experience what it is like to be here.

Give attention to the feelings, the sounds, what it smells like, how it tastes, what it feels like emotionally to be here.

Stop and touch something, **pay attention.**

- **We direct the movements of our consciousness through the act of paying attention.**

You can think of it in terms of having a light strapped to your forehead and you are in the darkness; where you turn and place your attention, THERE the light shines and you can see what there is. You can focus in on this to get more detail or widen your attention to take in more of the surroundings.

Paying attention is probably the hardest thing to learn as we are used to having our thoughts jump around from one thing to another; however, because the Sanctuary is so fascinating and OF COURSE CREATED ESPECIALLY FOR YOU by your own energy mind who knows you very well indeed, there will be always things that powerfully **draw your attention towards** them – and that makes it easy in Sanctuary to have your attention on the right things, at the right time.

The more attention you can pay, the more real and autogenic the habitat becomes, the more you enter into that world, and the easier it becomes to stay there.

You will experience moments at first where it becomes very real, like a lucid dream. At first, you'll probably flash in and out; but with experience, and most of all with practice, the energy stream will become steady, and much more rich and deep, and you get to stay in that amazing state of lucid awareness more and more.

Here are some tips to make it easier for you to get with the program and begin to develop your inborn abilities to experience autogenic environments in a lucid and fully associated way.

- **Describe what you see/hear/feel/experience OUT ALOUD.**

  This automatically and structurally creates a feedback loop in your physical brain that helps you to keep your attention, and keeps your conscious mind from dropping out of the party. If you feel stupid doing that, remember that if you don't want to STAY feeling stupid, speaking out aloud about what you see/ hear/ feel/ taste/ scent/ experience in Sanctuary is the best way forward!

- **Notice if you get wound up, stressed or frustrated...**

  ...and take a deep breath. Go back to where you "lost the plot" and re-group from there by saying, "Where was I? So the last thing I remember was that it was raining, and I felt cold, and..."

- **Ask many refining questions...**

  ...such as, "What else can I see? What else can I feel? What can I hear? What can I taste in my mouth? What scents can I detect in the air? How am I feeling about being here?" and answer out aloud.

- **Close your eyes and make the physical movements of reaching out or down and touching something.**

  Pay close attention to the feelings of your fingertips, in the palms of your hands. Say to yourself, "I want to feel this, let me feel this."

- **Don't be too hard on yourself when you first start.**

  It is easy but there are various tricks and skills to it, and most people are thoroughly rusty when it comes to lucid awareness and full body autogenic experiences. Well, most people don't even have fully lucid "in body" experiences when they're **not** in Sanctuary!

And this brings me to my last and extremely important tip for beginners.

When you're **not** in Sanctuary, i.e. as you are going about your daily life, stop numerous times in the course of the day and ask yourself, "What do I see/ hear/ taste/ scent/ feel/ experience right now?"

- **Pay some attention to your general environment in that focused way, become AWARE of what is happening in you, with you and around you – you could think of it in terms of "lucid living" or being "lucidly aware".**

Those are exactly the same skills that you need to play well in Sanctuary too.

Finally:

➢ **Allow yourself to be fascinated by the process.**

Your very own energy mind created this entire for you; it created the season, the weather, every tree, bush, leaf, rock, every grain of sand, every cloud in the sky and raindrop that falls. It made an organic energy tapestry - a matrix - for you to read and move about in.

It created a dwelling for you.

Take your time and look at the dwelling. Walk towards it. Touch it, look at the details of its structure, extend all your senses to describe it out aloud so it becomes more and more real in every sense of the word.

Now, find the door or entrance to the dwelling.

Take a moment to really take in the reality of the entrance and how to open it. Make the movements with your body to help you get "into it" and encourage your mind to really let you step across and into the Sanctuary world.

Enter your dwelling, go inside and explore it.

What rooms are there, what is inside these rooms?

Are there any objects that take your attention?

We call objects that are placed into a habitat by your energy mind and that stand out to you as interesting or even quite strange **artefacts.**

These artefacts are often very important messages, portals to other information, shaped like that, to draw your attention and to get you to do something with these special objects, **to invite you to play WITH THAT.**

For example, your dwelling might have a room with a table and chair.

Nothing too unusual there, you might think. But then you notice that on the table sits a strange statue of a frog made from green stone.

That is clearly an artefact, and now you could go and interact with it. What is it for? Pick it up. Hold it. How does it make you feel? What is the purpose of it? Where did it come from?

What am I supposed to do with this???

This is what we call a **Project Sanctuary puzzle**.

The energy mind has sent a message, and we consciously now have to work out what it means. Sometimes this is easy and we have an immediate idea or intuition what to do next. Sometimes it is extremely perplexing and very frustrating because we can't seem to get it or work it out.

But don't despair.

The most important thing to remember about Project Sanctuary is this:

- **Project Sanctuary is MAGIC MANIFEST.**

It is completely energetic; all things are made from nothing but energy data and that means that everything is fluid and everything can change for the sake of a single thought.

<u>YOU have all the magic</u>, all the knowledge, all the resources of time and space at your command here.

That is the most difficult thing for beginners to remember, because we bring our conscious limitations, all our beliefs and all our errors of judgement with us when we enter Sanctuary.

In Sanctuary, we are not just “old Mr Smith” or “dumb Patsy” or “useless loser Sam” or whatever we think of ourselves to be.

- **We are MAGIC INCARNATE.**

We just need to remember this!

And something that does help us in this enormous and central task is our friends – our guides, our advisers, our messengers and bridges so we can talk to the energy mind directly, like you would talk to another person and get answers and help that we might consciously understand.

So let us ask for help and a friend to manifest, someone who we can trust absolutely, someone who loves us deeply and cares for us, someone who is the perfect entity to help us make sense of these new and wonderful realms with their language of light, events, objects, landscapes and artefacts.

Who is this friend for you?

Answer the following questions out aloud.

Don't think about it, simply take the very first answer that pops into your mind, accept it and use it to add more and more information data to this construct until the threshold shift occurs and the friend becomes “real”.

Co-Create A Friend With Your Energy Mind

Answer the questions out aloud.

- Is it human?
- Male or female?
- What does it look like?
- What are they wearing?
- What is particularly interesting or unusual about them?
- When they speak, what does it sound like?
- When you are in their presence, how do you feel?

Take time to say hello and get comfortable with your friend. Go for a walk with them, talk to them, tell them about yourself, about your hopes and dreams, and by all means, ask about theirs. The more you know about each other, the better you can work and play together, and the better your results will be all around.

Do take your time.

The beauty of these stable habitats is that the room with the table and chairs and the green frog stone statue aren't going anywhere. You'll find your way back there again at any time. This puzzle will be waiting for you until you are ready to solve it.

This is also a very interesting and important thing to know about Project Sanctuary and the energy mind.

In the past, the so called subconscious or unconscious mind was deemed to be fickle and unreliable, insane, weird, uncontrollable, unpredictable.

The habitats show us that the energy mind is no such thing.

On the contrary, it is completely logical but different from what we might have learned in conscious school.

The energy mind is complex, beautiful, logical and also completely stable.

The house and the frog will remain; they are there, they're not melting or morphing – they are waiting for you.

In my example, the person talked with their friend and the friend made a comment which triggered the memory of a fairy tale whereby a princess kisses a frog to transform it into a prince.

Armed with this new insight, the person rushed back to the house, picked up the artefact, kissed it – and it transformed into a young man they had had a super intense first love relationship with when they were a teenager.

The person in question was really astonished by this. They couldn't work out why their energy mind had sent this of all things as the first thing to deal with in Sanctuary; but the young man was there, and they had a talk about their first love and something important was accomplished there, even though it is difficult if not impossible to put into words what that might have been.

➢ **It is a very important rule of playing Project Sanctuary to not try and analyse, or psycho-analyse, what goes on in the stories and events.**

That gets us no-where and more importantly, it takes us away from the core and spirit of Sanctuary – remember, we don't develop by thinking "about" this and that, but ONLY by playing the game.

It is good enough, more than good enough, that the young man was there, that they talked and hugged, that he left happily with an open invitation to return any time he wants to; and the frog puzzle was solved successfully.

The player in question was awed by their experience and also extremely grateful and delighted to have had it; they couldn't really say exactly WHAT that did for them, but they could FEEL it made a huge difference on many different levels.

With the threshold shift established, now, we can move on.

We can discover more things, ask questions, get on to the next exploration in this habitat, or any other we might choose.

We might change some things, make a garden, expand the house, install features we want such as a healing shower or a good luck bed to sleep in; we might invite people to come visit us there; we may create portals to other worlds; we may practise basic Sanctuary skills such as flying, or changing an object into something else.

- **The first habitat is very much a total playground just for you in every sense of the word.**

If you are very driven about your healing, spiritual development, intellectual development, psychic development, business success and so forth, you might have to take yourself in hand and prescribe a schedule of fun, rest, relaxation and exploration for at least 50% of the time you spend in this habitat. This is the perfect place to let go of all sorts of pressures you put upon yourself just for a moment and re-discover the joy of life, and love of life, that is natural in all of us.

- **Remember that Project Sanctuary is pure energy – and energy is flowing, light and playful by nature.**

Everything in Project Sanctuary, including what the astral body that you use to walk and talk there looks like, all the things, events, objects and entities are all made from energy data and therefore, are infinitely malleable.

Everything can be changed and morphed at will.

- You can melt a rock, turn a frog into a prince, or solidify a fountain into a diamond sculpture.
- You can fly or move from one place to another in the blink of an eye, or the wiggle of your nose if that's what you decide to use.
- You can move through time, backwards and forwards, and sideways as well.
- You can be as small as an atom and as big as a galaxy if you choose so you can take in a different perspective on the situation.

- You can side step into different dimensions, and one of the most useful is the pattern world, where you see people, trees and buildings not in their normal pictures, but like meshes of light and colour, like a multidimensional tapestry and then it is easy to spot where things have gone wrong or something needs to be repaired.

- You can wave a magic wand, or have a magical friend to do the magic for you – this and so much more is at your disposal.

All you need to do to activate the real magic of the Sanctuary realms and the human mind is to remember that even though things seem to be hard and real, they are only living metaphors - everything is made out of energy, or as we say, “It's ONLY energy!”

It's Only Energy - Avoiding Magic Failure

It happens sometimes that we get so involved with a story that we forget the nature of the game, everything becomes "hard" and we might find ourselves sitting in front of a big mountain and wail because we can't see any way to climb this.

This state we call "magic failure" - the person who is wailing in front of the "impossibly high mountain" has simply forgotten for the moment that they could think themselves to the other side, or to the top in an instance; that they could fly by themselves, ride a dragon, get a helicopter, tunnel underneath the mountain or make the whole mountain disappear **at will**!

Should this happen to you, don't worry. Magic failure is an amazing thing that happens to the best of us, and not just in Project Sanctuary.

Magic failure is simply a form of structural energy system collapse that happens when we think the wrong thoughts, such as "I can't do this," "This is too difficult," or "I'm not good enough," etc. and simply makes those statements become perfectly real by making us forget that we have all the magic in all the worlds and **what we think and say actually really does create reality.**

Magic failure is only a sign of stress, and if you remind yourself that "this is only energy!" on a regular basis, you will find you can take a deep sigh of relief, and sanity and logic will return to you. When that happens, all our Creator given systems of mind, body and spirit come back online, and as soon as they do, all our choices, resources, intelligence, logic, experience and powers come flooding back to us.

This includes knowing that **there is no Sanctuary puzzle that you can't solve**, and that your energy mind wouldn't even have sent you this particular challenge if it didn't know that you're up to solving it.

Now here's the last important aspect of the marvellous space of freedom that is Sanctuary you need to know about before we start.

The Threshold Shifts

When you have solved a puzzle, played a story through to its natural conclusion, completed a quest or a rescue mission, received a flash vision that is that moment of the creative lightning strike, you experience a particular movement of the mind, body and energy system we call "**a threshold shift**".

This is a physically noticeable "Aha!" or "Wow!" or "Eureka!!" moment, where something special happens and you know that you have learned something new, understood something about yourself or the universe at large, or to be more precise, **that you have changed** in some way.

- **The story is not complete until there has been a threshold shift – indeed, <u>the threshold shift is the purpose of the story.</u>**

In the example story about the green frog, the person experienced their first threshold shift occurred when they "kissed the frog" and later on, the most intense threshold shift of the story happened as they sat talking with the young man, holding hands, looking into each other's eyes and acknowledging to each other how precious and wonderful their first love had been.

Threshold shifts are typically very, very ***moving*** – quite literally, a lot of energy is moved through the systems that may have been stuck for decades in an instance, and they leave the person who experiences that in a state of great clarity and peace, often intense delight and joy as well.

As the energy system itself, through the energy mind, is what is drawing your attention to certain issues or blockages or unresolved issues, this is a very safe system where you are only ever working with things that are important to you personally, and you are also working towards Even Flow, resolution, healing, expansion of consciousness, evolution – **<u>your threshold shifts are IN THE RIGHT DIRECTION and in accordance with your own highest personal path.</u>**

This makes Project Sanctuary completely unique and set apart from all other methods of therapy, healing, mental, intellectual, psychic, spiritual and personal development – **it is tailored by you for you, and you work with your own personal threshold shifts every time you step into a story, every time you play the game.**

When you feel you know enough to play on behalf of another, so that they can have an amazing and transformative Project Sanctuary experience of their very own, then it will be perfectly tailored through you for them – your energy mind gets in touch with theirs, they have a communication, and you can inform both of you of the results by telling the story you see, explaining the vision, and, if necessary, changing it together for the highest good of all concerned.

So with this short overview of the Project Sanctuary main building blocks, you have enough to start taking a journey to a Sanctuary of your own, and start playing the ultimate game in space and time for real, and for yourself.

Introducing The Genius Symbols

Now I am going to introduce the Project Sanctuary derived Genius Symbols.

These are very, very simple symbols which serve as portals to structurally replace asking the questions we were talking about earlier.

The symbols make it easy to connect up with the energy mind because there is no extra translation with speech involved to get a **flash vision** in response to the symbol; more symbols can then be used to refine the vision into a full habitat with its events, adventures – and eventual threshold shifts.

I have developed these symbols in co-operation with my energy mind and with that of others over a period of time to create a kind of basic alphabet to open the doors of communication between the conscious mind and the energy mind.

- **Each symbol is a portal in its own right.**

One of the really interesting features of the Genius Symbols is that you can use them and understand them at any logical level you want to play, from the utterly mundane to the super-meta abstract.

So for example, the time symbol can remind you that you have to buy an alarm clock when you go into town later that day, but it can also denote an incredibly complex time sculpture, such as a person's many incarnations in context and everything in between – depending on your contract, on where YOU want to play on any given day.

Your contract sets the logical level at which your answer will arrive.

Logical Levels & The Genius Symbols

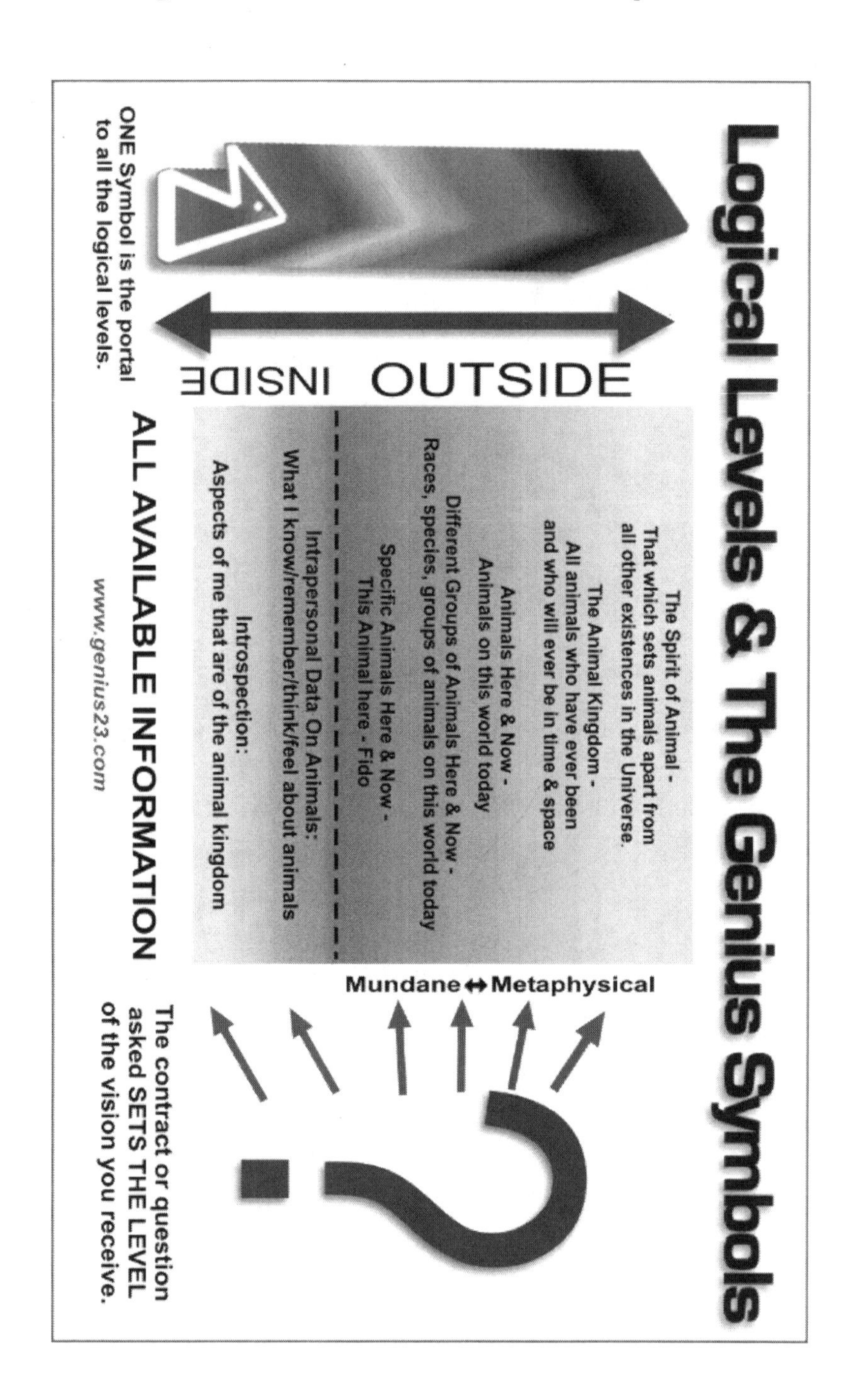

Each symbol exists at all logical levels, from the very specific here-and-now to the extremely abstract, metaphysical, spiritual, global, which is one of the hallmarks of metaphor/unconscious/energy mind communication and has caused much confusion to people working with unconsciously generated materials and visions in the past.

For example, the time symbol can be about such things as the Lord of Time itself, the Zeitgeist, the structure of time in the Universe at large. It can also refer to the way people measure and understand time; to the seasons, the hours in the day, and all the way down to the actual clock on your bedside table that might have run out of batteries, causing you to be late for work tomorrow.

It is understandable that in the past, when people worked with symbols and metaphors and most importantly, with communications from their own energy mind, they got confused amongst the logical levels, hopelessly lost and so the information received made no sense, because **the reference of which logical level it was relating to**, was absent.

In the Genius Symbols, what we do to end this logical levels confusion is to decide up front which logical level we are seeking an answer at, and pitching a question, a contract or a set up at that specific logical level.

So for example, with the people symbol, we might ask for something that...

- is global to all people by virtue of structure;
- or we might seek a more specific answer or solution for people alive in the world today;
- or in a particular country,
- or in a city,
- or in this particular business,
- or in a department of this one business,
- or of a particular family,

- or for this one particular person,
- or even further down, for an aspect[2] of one single person.

The question or contract sets the logical level for the answer to be understood at.

This makes the Genius Symbols unique; and in deciding up front at which level you are seeking the information you are seeking from the energy mind, you find out (usually much to people's amazement!) that their energy mind can handle all these logical levels with ease and most importantly, with surprising **accuracy and specificity** - something that was previously entirely unheard of when working with unconsciously generated materials, memories and visions.

Also, thinking about the logical levels you're pitching your question or contracts at **before** you ask the question or create the contract is very good training in the arts of working correctly with the logical levels of any situation or problem, or even problem group.

The way this works with "real people in the real world" is that the distinction made is not that of abstraction VS specificity, but of metaphysical VS mundane instead.

For example, someone might ask their energy mind, "What would be the perfect colour for my aura to be at this important party tonight?" which is an esoteric or metaphysical question, a very complex metaphor that describes overall state across the board - for an "aura" to be a particular colour, a person's emotions, physical state, thought, behaviour all have to align in a highly specific way.

Or they might ask, "What colour should my tie be tonight?" which is extremely mundane as the energy mind in response flashes up the green tie with the purple stripes, one single specific object our friend actually has in his wardrobe.

---

[2] An aspect of a person is a snapshot of the whole person at a particular moment in time. Everyone has infinite aspects but they are easy to separate and deal with if taken quite literally, one at a time. The aspects model replaces the old parts model as a more workable way of describing different states with corresponding differences in beliefs, emotions and behaviours a single human being inhabits sequentially through time. See *Events Psychology*.

The movement of going up the logical levels towards more abstract and **inclusive** themes, metaphors, existences gives likewise more leverage, the higher up you go, over all the systems that are lower down the logical levels.

In NLP, the movement of going towards more abstraction is called "chunking up" and the movement into more specificity or the more mundane is called "chunking down".

As an aside, the ability to move smoothly around the logical levels of any given system is essential for real intelligence; and the entrained human propensity to only ever chunk down into more and more details, which leads to less and less leverage and control over the system as a whole, is a real stumbling block to applying intelligence and finding intelligent solutions to the problems that have been created by low chunk, details orientated, "narrow minded" and overly hard thinking in the first place.

At the beginning of this chapter you saw a diagram illustrating an example of moving around the logical levels of a single genius symbol, which is a form of level-free metaphor or **gateway to all the information** that we can gain by adding the input of the energy mind to the data the conscious mind has assembled and organised, thus often exponentially increasing the amount of information on any given topic, which is what leads to the new ideas and the genius solutions in the first place.

As you can see:

- **By controlling the logical levels through the contract, we essentially unlock all the information that exists throughout all the logical levels of that one symbol.**

This is a single symbol example; of course, things become far more multi-dimensional and fun when you start combining symbols. But even with all 23 symbols in play for a single question or contract, we still keep a steady course by using the question to hold all this vast amount of information together and sort for what we need to know in order to do exactly what we want to be doing.

Understanding how logical levels work is at the very least, one of the master keys of understanding systems within systems, understanding relationships, ecology, and "seeing the bigger picture".

It is particularly important so that we do not get lost amidst the logical levels, and don't end up applying mundane or low chunk strategies when something much more abstract, metaphysical or high level is required to solve a problem - and vice versa.

For someone working with the Genius Symbols, it can also be observed what kinds of questions are routinely being asked, and where these questions are pitched at in the overall system that contains all the logical levels.

Some people have a tendency to always go for the very abstract or esoteric realms which may not always be the most effective place to leverage a system, or achieve a result. Likewise, people who have a tendency to be very "narrow minded" and unable to “see the bigger picture” will begin to notice after a while and expand their thinking to include and involve higher chunk questions, at least once in a while.

This brings flexibility back into our systems of thinking and information sorting and processing, and best of all, creates much better "matches" between the problems we have and the solutions we find for them.

When you come to make these symbols for your own use, you will be accepting them both consciously as well as unconsciously in an agreement that this is how we are going to open these doors of communication.

In the later sections we will discuss how you make the symbols your own and the various ways in which to use the symbols; here, we will simply and briefly meet the 23 Genius Symbols so that you can recognise them when you see them again.

Space

The simple square or box is the symbol for space.

When we play a classic Project Sanctuary game, this is the first symbol we place, and we use this symbol to make our statement of intent for the experience, state our set up. This symbol takes us to the "Project Sanctuary Space" - the realms where all these amazing things are going to happen.

In general layouts and if you draw this symbol, space includes many things such as distance, and size; location and relative position of objects also belongs to the space symbol. if this symbol turns up in a reading or a pattern, it encourages you to play with the space aspects of a story.

There are many important ways in which we can take charge and make use of space in Sanctuary. **Zoom movements** such as allowing yourself to grow in size as large as you need to be to really get a good overview, see the bigger picture, or even feel safe in a fight with an enemy; or conversely shrinking yourself down to walk in the matrix of a crystal or live on an atom that has become a planet are extremely freeing for the mind and often very important to solve a problem.

The space symbol reminds us that we have the power to place things where we want them; to have them any size we want them to be, and to travel any distance in the blink of an eye. Relating to ourselves, space denotes our ability to extend, reach and stretch out, travel, effect and reach things on all levels and including spiritual, mental, emotional and physical.

Time

In the classic game, the first active symbol is for time – remember we ask, “What is the time of day, what is the time of year?” to get the time co-ordinates to our habitat fixed, be this in a vision or in a memory.

You can think of the shape as an hourglass, or an upright infinity symbol to help you remember that this is the symbol for time.

When you draw (random) this symbol in a layout or pattern, it asks you to pay attention to the time aspect of the story or puzzle, and might be advising that if you move in time, you'll better understand what's going on, so this symbol might indicate time travel, or a connection with time in a different way, for example past lives, or future ones.

As humans in our societies at present, we have very limiting ideas of time and that's one place where we get stuck a lot – by trying to hold back the tides of time, or make it move faster or slower, or simply by thinking that we are stuck in time like flies in a river of honey and there's nothing we can do about it.

The ability to move through and with time freely, backwards, forwards and sideways, up and down as well, is one of the most freeing abilities for the human mind, which in truth does not have any temporal limitations at all.

Weather

The little cloud is the symbol for weather. If you remember, in the classic game we ask after the time of day for the weather next.

The weather is a metaphor for many things, influences of the environment that are crucial to the unfoldment of a story.

If you have ever seen a weather map or a satellite image of planet Earth, with these moving systems of clouds that bring wind and rain, or sunshine and snow, cold or warm, misty or dry, and you consider the effects the weather has on any habitat, you'll get a sense of how important that is.

For healing endeavours for example, it is crucial to have the right weather; for many stories to create a change in the weather can bring about the most profound threshold shifts.

When this symbol turns up you are asked to pay attention to the weather aspects of your story or puzzle, and/or to work with the weather more intimately.

On a wider metaphorical level, the weather symbol relates to the systems within us that produce energy for life, change, and all emotions.

And then there are the really big unfoldments like galactic weather, sun storms, and including astrology.

Land

The two mountains (or an island in the ocean, if you will) symbol stands for the land – the landscape in which your story is set, the primary environment that materially holds your story together, the world in which it plays or as we would say, the underlying structure of the habitat you're in.

If you get the landscape symbol in the reading, it directs your attention to the physical structures that hold your habitat together, and to look more closely there for answers.

The land includes also deserts, rivers and oceans, alien landscapes too, and remember that landscapes, even tall mountains, flow and change through time; that is an important aspect of their nature.

On a wider level, the land further includes the galaxies, the stars in the sky, the whole planet, the solar system you're in, astrological influences and much more.

"The Land" in its widest metaphorical sense is the physical manifestation of the Universe.

As a personal metaphor, the land relates to the most basic structures of our own physical manifestations and energy systems.

Plant

The little tree is the symbol for the plant kingdom. We take this generally completely for granted, but the plant kingdom underlies all life on Earth and is the backbone of all we think of when we think of "nature".

The plant kingdom and vegetation in a habitat are immensely important; like all things in Sanctuary, the kinds of plants you find there, from the smallest mushroom to the most beautiful flower and greatest and stateliest tree these are very specific components of the energy stream, energy cocktail.

In a general reading, the tree symbol for plants directs your attention to the plant kingdom and to investigate there for solutions and forward momentum.

As with all Project Sanctuary symbols, there is this "as above, so below" aspect.

There are systems and circuitry within each human being that resonate at that level of pure green nature and are touched and healed only by that.

Animal

The animal shape stands for all the animal kingdom, from the smallest spider and snail to the most impressive killer whale spirit animal and beyond to the spirit we call the Lord of the Animals overall.

Animals are obviously very important to the overall ecology of a story; but traditionally and metaphorically they are also used as messengers, guides and support from a very specific and powerful strata that exists within us just the same.

The animal symbol asks you to consider how the animal kingdom is of help or involved in your story, or relevant in your enquiry.

On a wider metaphorical level, the animal symbol also denotes those levels of ourselves which belong to that kingdom, our animal nature and animal instincts and drives.

Crystal

In geology, crystals are lumped in with all forms of minerals; in metaphysics, they are in a class of their own, form their own kingdom which has a different level of existence than bedrock, sandstone or granite.

Crystals can be extremely important catalysts and can act as messengers, doorways, power sources and much beside.

The crystal symbol also encompasses the crystalline dimensions of pure logic and absolute order, timeless, perfect and immutable.

If the crystal turns up in your reading, it asks you to pay attention to messages from and through that domain, to look at the logic, the underlying structure, to leave emotional disturbances out of it and be "crystal clear" about the cause and effect of the situation. Don't think of this crystal clear logic as loveless however; there is a place where love and logic become one and the same and to enter there is one of the most powerful human experiences possible.

Metaphorically relating to ourselves, the crystal is the symbol for the levels of your existence which are of that vibration.

Angel

The angel symbol stands for higher beings and higher forces of all kinds which are having an interest or even a direct guiding hand in the unfoldments of your story.

I also refer to these higher forces as “the powers that be” to exclude no-one, and to include also aspects of our own mind, soul and self which may reside on a higher level which is generally out of the reach of the conscious mind (but often felt, and noted nonetheless!).

Apart from that, the angel symbol also denotes your God/s, highest spiritual beings, and all those you pray to.

Friend

Friends is the term we use for spirit guides, helpful entities, invisible friends and all sorts of potential helpers and advisers which we can turn to ask for help and assistance.

Having good friends, and having deep and meaningful personal relationships with them is central to success in Sanctuary as friends act as a bridge between your conscious self and the energy realms at large.

Unlike people or angels who have their own agenda, friends are absolutely there for you and absolutely on your side – they walk beside you and have no other purpose than to help YOU, unconditionally.

If the friend symbol, a little person wearing a kind of robe, turns up in a reading, you are advised to involve your existing friends, or bring in a new one to help you on this mission.

When this symbol refers back to you or another human, it can ask if you are acting as a friend – a champion, in your/their highest and best interest.

It can also denote that you are to act as an unconditional friend or champion on behalf of an aspect, or yourself.

People

The “little man” sign stands for all kinds of people: real people from your life, people who may inhabit a habitat, fairy people, dwarves, elves and alien people as well.

When you find the people sign in a reading, you are asked to pay attention to the intelligent and active beings in the environment and how you are interacting with them on the “people” level.

When this symbol refers back to you, it might ask you to consider if you are currently acting and appreciating yourself as a human being.

Spirit

The ghost sign stands for spirits, dead people, people from the other side, ancestors and so forth.

Spirits can be invisible if you just look at the surface and if this symbol turns up in a reading, you need to take account of that realm because there is something relevant there for you.

In the wider metaphorical sense, "the spirit of a thing" is a quality that sometimes is quite different from what you see with your eyes of day alone; this can apply to any thing, person, or situation as well.

Aspect

Each individual person has many "aspects" to them which all work together to make more than the sum of their parts, like the many facets of a diamond which may appear in many different colours; that is why the sign for aspects is shaped like a triangle, a facet of the diamond that is you.

Aspects can personify certain traits or ideas; aspects can also be from a time past, and even from a past or future life.

If the aspect sign turns up in a reading, pay attention to which aspect/s of you are most involved in this story or puzzle as they may hold the key to the solution.

Most if not all things have aspects of their own; the aspect symbol can ask you to consider different sides of the story, or shift your point of view to see a bigger picture of which the aspect currently in front of you is only a part.

House

Houses, buildings, shelters, house boats, huts, tents – any kind of dwelling comes with the sign of the little house.

Dwellings are man (or other being) made shelters or other types of artificial environments and of course, all the rooms and lower logical level subdivisions that exist there.

In many dream books and symbol books of old, it is thought that the house is a symbol of the body; this is not so because the body is made by the Creative Order, it is clearly not man made.

As such, in the wider metaphorical sense and in terms of people, the house symbol denotes the conscious self construct, a man made idea of the self or body instead.

Artefact

The sign for artefacts is a cup but of course, an artefact can be any kind of object. Artefacts are portals to complete realms, doorways to other related streams of events.

The energy mind has ways to help you spot an artefact – whether it is something intriguing to you that draws your attention; whether it is something that glows or something that is ridiculously out of place in an environment, you'll know an artefact when you find one.

When the cup symbol for artefacts turns up in your reading, have a look around for a special object. Sometimes a quest is required to find it.

Artefacts also work the other way around – they are the manifestation in physical form of an underlying energetic information set.

The artefact symbol can therefore also denote that an idea must be made "hard" or to manifest something material that will serve as a portal for further unfoldments.

The Gift

The box with the diagonal lines is the sign for The Gift. A gift can be anything at all, from an entire planet to a tiny flower, given to a person, a friend, a situation, a habitat to make it happier, better, more joyous or more functional.

Ask, "What kind of gift can I give to this?" and let something come to you. Remember it is a complex energy cocktail packaged in the form of The Gift so you can handle it, and give and receive it.

You can also ask that a The Gift be given to you or the situation at hand by someone else.

The Gift is just that – a gift. It is very essentially NOT an exchange by nature but something that is given without having to earn it, work for it, make it happen somehow or having to pay something back for it.

It is like a pulse that seeks no return, unconditional in nature.

Therefore, this symbol also stands for what you might call a miracle.

Giving gifts is easy. To receive them with grace is often a far greater challenge.

Trade

The two coins symbol denotes Pertineri Market or trade in general.

Pertineri Market is an intergalactic, interdimensional market place where all manner of beings come together for trade; it is a shared Project Sanctuary habitat outside that can be used to trade in resources, find help, or disperse one's own contributions.

Trading is about an exchange of energies so that a balance is achieved that pleases both (or more) parties and brings them both equal benefits; so the two coins trade symbol asks us to pay attention to all forms of trades and exchanges in the widest sense as well.

Dragonwings

The Dragonwings symbol asks us to shift our attention to the bigger picture, the pattern world, the structure or tapestry of the story.

In the pattern world, things look very different and many times it is much easier to see what's wrong or where the problems lie. The pattern world also often reveals "invisible" components or influences of a story.

"Rising above" the current situation, drawing a mental or physical map of the story and placing all the main components in relation to each other can be a good way for beginners to start viewing events in a different way and to discern the underlying deeper and larger patterns, understand the bigger picture.

Magic

A very important Project Sanctuary symbol is that of magic, the spiral.

All of Project Sanctuary is pure magic, but how well it works and how good our results are individually relies on how much we can manage to REMEMBER THAT when we play the stories.

Coming into the game with our prejudices, and often in magic failure, we generally fail to use even a small percentage of the pure magic on offer in Sanctuary, and this symbol reminds us to increase the magic – exponentially, if you can mentally handle it.

Magic blows out the limitations to our perceptions and thinking which was entrained in the every day/hard/physical world and allows us to get to grips with actual reality which consists in truth of the physical world plus.

Stardust

Three little stars, or perhaps snow flakes, are the symbol for stardust.

There is a level of existence where all is pure potential – tiny sparks of glittering pre-light in a velvet space of black that holds the potential for all things.

Sprinkling a little stardust (or fairy dust, if you will!) on any situation will create a re-connection to that realm, and the incredible potential of any situation becomes revealed.

There is of course a very personal level at which we are all made of stardust absolute.

Alien

There is more to the Universe than we people have so far experienced here on Earth, and when we come across the alien symbol we are asked to remember that what we think of as perfectly reasonable and rational may just be so because we're used to our local conventions and nothing else – for example, the only reason we think of metal as hard and cold is because of our local conventions of temperature and gravity we are so used to that we tend to forget things are quite different, elsewhere.

We can stretch our incredible, infinite minds to take a new perspective and thus understand important knowledge about the greater Universe.

This symbol can also practically denote travel to alien worlds, making contact with alien visitors, or alien influences in general.

Fountain

The fountain symbol stands for pure creative energy, the wellsprings of our existence, the pure and unstoppable creative force that powers the Universe itself.

If this symbol turns up in a story, bring in the energy of pure creativity, let literally the creativity burst forth like a fountain from the bedrock of old to bring new life to all it touches.

The Dance

EVERYTHING is a dance – action and reaction, movement and counter-movement, ebb and flow.

This dance is always beautiful, always joyous.

The two intertwined waves symbol of the dance asks us what we can do to improve our recognition of the dance, and how we can further it in any given situation.

This symbol is also about movement and evolution; being light on your feet so you can get out of ruts that you might have become stuck in.

You need at least two to tango. The dance reminds us that things don't happen in isolation, that there is cause & effect and that we have to take both or more parties into consideration if we want to solve problems.

It is also extremely important to remember that dancing isn't work, but it is JOYOUS – an expression of life, and love of life.

Light

The star or sun or light flash stands for the light – that which brings life to all, that which de-lights us, that which can shed light on many situations, which can en-lighten us and if we live in it, we experience pure joy and ecstasy of being.

This symbol can ask us to look at a situation in a more enlightened fashion, see the light within, and be light - as opposed to being dour, heavy and grim.

Adding some extra light to any situation can reveal much, and heal much, as well as explain almost anything...

Making Your Own Personal Genius Symbol Set

It is essential to the process of playing with and drawing visions through the Genius Symbols that you make your own symbol set or sets as the act of **drawing the symbols** is a very special form of learning the symbols, accepting them, making them your own.

- **When you draw, paint, engrave the symbols WITH YOUR OWN Hand they become YOUR OWN symbols from that moment forth.**

You can draw the symbols on pieces of paper or on card; my favourite way of making a symbol set is to select individual stones as they are very tactile and the whole process of choosing and then dedicating the stone to a symbol is extremely meditative and also magical in nature.

My own first set was drawn in metallic marker on beach pebbles; I still have it and sometimes I still use it when I am drawn to it.

Since then I have gone on to make many more and different types of Genius Symbol sets, including small ones that are easy to carry on travels and journeys; showy ones using dichroic cabochons; a nice set made by cutting through a branch of a birch tree to make circular slices and then polished to be silky smooth; a set of clay symbols and one made from wooden dice with only one symbol on one side and five blank sides so you can throw the dice and get only certain symbols to reveal themselves.

Other people who have sent in pictures of their symbol sets have made them from glass pebbles, bone, rose quartz and hematite, wooden discs, sea shells and many other materials they personally found attractive and were drawn to.

You can use any material that calls you or that you discover to be perfect for you; this can change through time as well but please remember that the most important thing are the symbols themselves, and you can and will have fabulous experiences and marvellous results, even if your symbols are drawn on a few scraps of paper with the charcoaled end of a burned twig.

There is a caveat to this, however.

The Genius Symbols are truly a "whole person experience". We think about them with our conscious mind, and use them to communicate with the energy mind. We draw them with our physical hands and hold and touch them, they are physically real.

From experience with many Genius Symbol students I have learned that **the more a person likes their own symbol sets, the better their results become.**

People who took my comment that you can "draw the symbols on scraps of paper and they will still work" as an excuse to be lazy, not to bother with finding some attractive, tactile templates such as glass pebbles, stones, crystals, sea shells and such and instead used "bits of a ripped up cornflake box" did not get the same results as those who loved their templates, loved their own personal Genius Symbol sets and found them **highly attractive**.

The attractiveness of your own symbol set is clearly a highly important additional device to help you keep the focus, to make you want to interact with your symbol set, to admire it, and of course, to create a powerful **personal relationship** with your own symbol set and all the individual symbols within it.

Should you ever find yourself stranded on a lonely island, incarcerated in a dungeon, or lost in space, yes, you can still make Genius Symbol sets out of all and every materials you can glean from an impoverished environment.

For the purposes of unlocking your own genius and creativity however, and living in a civilised environment, I highly recommend you make the effort and find templates for your symbols that are at least respectful, and preferably, highly attractive to your own good self.

Making the symbol set your own can take many forms; some people like to decorate and make works of art out of the symbols.

This is entirely up to you but do try and keep the **focus on the simplicity** of the symbols and don't overwhelm them with too much external decorations or confusing energetic additions that may take away from their simple, clear power.

Learning The Genius Symbols

Draw the symbols large into the air in front of you, using your hands, and say their names.

Take a moment to reflect if you get a sense of what this symbol is all about.

If you know how to do EmoTrance, you might ET your responses until the symbol flows smoothly in, through and out and you feel good, fully energised, tingling, and you are aware of the actual feel of the energy of this symbol in your body.

If a symbol scares you, feels weird or as though "I really don't need this one... ever..." you might need to do some extra work on this.

For EmoTrancers, you know what to do; you can also use EFT and tap on your feelings with the usual opening statements that would arise.

You can also meditate on the symbols that caused an adverse reaction or play a classic game to discover more about the causes of your responses to a particular symbol.

- **Don't be worried if you "don't understand a symbol completely".**

I certainly don't!

Every one of them has so many levels, layers, so much depth, is a portal to so much more, I would be surprised if any of us ever got the bottom of a single one and "what it really means".

A sense that you have touched the energy and recognised it, even vaguely, and just enough so you can tell the difference between the symbols is more than good enough to get started.

The depth and richness of your personal visions as you play your own games and gain your own threshold shifts is not affected by whether you understand the symbols or not. The symbols just open the door and your energy mind will do the rest.

There is much merit spending a day or two with a single symbol, to carry it with you and let it trigger memories, thoughts, ideas, flashes and visions.

I like to “make friends with” those things I work with and I seek to understand because I find when I am friends with something, a connection arises through which information travels much more freely.

Taking a symbol or two out and about with you and giving it some extra attention will certainly pay off in the long run.

Choosing Your Templates

As I have mentioned, my first symbol set was made from beach pebbles.

It took me a surprising amount of time to find all 23 on the beach that day, even though the beach is of course, covered in literally millions of pebbles.

I let my feelings and attention guide me where they wanted me to go and even though it took a while, eventually I had my 23 templates.

I suggest you go and get yours as soon as possible. If there are no natural sources of pebbles and stones in your area, you can get packs of pebbles from home furnishing stores, new age shops and at a very cut rate price from garden centres. Aquarium shops too have often interesting pebbles of many different kinds and colours available.

Bring your templates home and if they can take it, place them in a bowl of salt water for a day and a night out in the open where the sun and the moon can shine on them. This will clear them and make them ready for your use as your personal first symbol deck.

Applying The Symbols

I don't know about you, but my hands aren't 100% steady and I often produce a "wiggly line" when I wanted to draw a straight one.

Also, natural stones and even glass pebbles have dips and dents in them which make it difficult, if not impossible, to produce "perfect symbols" like the ones I created in a computer drawing program for this manual!

Really, do not worry about it. Practise drawing all the symbols a few times on paper first, then on a comparable surface.

I use permanent markers and metallic markers; but you can also apply the symbols with a brush.

Some of them are a little harder to replicate than others, but as tests show, even a five year old could do them on the first try to the degree that the adults in the room were perfectly able to recognise which symbol each one was supposed to be.

And THAT is the main purpose – for you to be able to see and **recognise the symbol**.

In fact, that's their only purpose.

So if your symbols are a bit wonky, don't worry about it. It makes truly no difference to your energy mind if your angel ended up with a bit of a tail; it knows what you were trying to do, and the symbol will work perfectly well for you.

So and when you are ready, you've practised with your medium, and you have made sure the templates/stones are really dry and free of any oil or other slime, get your symbols list out, your pens and your templates, sit down somewhere comfortable, and simply pick up one at a time, hold it in your hand for a moment and say, "I dedicate you to (time)."

Place it down and draw the symbol as best you can; then place it to the side and say, "I have my symbol of (time)."

Choose the next stone/template and move on to the next symbol, repeating the above until all the symbols are done.

Now, place all the symbols in a circle - we call this the complete "symbol sphere".

Hold your hands over the completed symbol set and if you wish, you can tune in to the energy that the symbol sphere creates. You might light a candle and place in the center, and take some time out to simply sit with your new symbol set, let your thoughts flow freely and enjoy the fact that you have created a tool for yourself that will delight you, and surprise you in more ways than you can imagine just yet.

When you are done, your very own genius symbol set will be ready for your first game in space and time. **How exciting!**

Creating Visions With The Symbols

The Contract

There are two very different ways to play with the Genius Symbols and Sanctuary in general.

One form of playing a game, getting your vision, developing a story and obtaining threshold shifts is to **make a contract** - this is a request to the energy mind to provide something for a specific purpose.

An absolutely wonderfully healing example of working with a contract is to say loudly in your mind and with your voice at the same time:

"Dear energy mind, give me the perfect place in time and space for me right here, right now..."

The exquisite and extraordinary thing about this example is that the specific energies that the habitat contains are **calculated in real time** by your energy mind for you, so they are spot on appropriate for this movement exactly, every time.

There isn't a doctor or a chemist on Earth or anywhere else who could prescribe such a perfect tonic, a remedy that is so absolutely right for you, taking into consideration every personal and environmental variable possible and including time.

But your energy mind can.

This is a fabulously flexible resource you can use at any time, anywhere, and you will always get the right habitat, the right energies that will make you sigh with pleasure because it is so right for YOU – as you are, right now, and no matter what your state might be.

You can ask your energy mind anything you want using a contract:

"Take me to a memory that I need to heal today..."

"Give me a story for my 8 year old niece that will help her with her self esteem..."

"Give me a beautiful and powerful hypnotic journey for people who suffer from agoraphobia..."

"Show me where I'm stuck in this project!"

"Give me 23 ideas how to make more money!"

"Give me some thing for this headache..."

The last version, where I highlighted the word **some thing**, is the most user-friendly contract of them all – we leave it up to the energy mind just what it will give us or what form that will take.

It could be a thought, a long story, an insight, a single symbol, a feeling, a habitat, a reminder, a memory – anything really. We just tell the energy mind what we want the **some thing** for (X) or (X and Y and Z), and it calculates the rest, based on its in depth knowledge of ALL of our systems.

Amazing.

We all have so many unfulfilled needs and wants, so many things we wish were different, hopes and dreams and worries too about all these things, for ourselves and other people, that many people only work with very specific contracts up front, all the time.

But that's a shame because a lot of our problems, if we were to step outside of them for a just a moment, learn something we didn't even know we needed to learn, or get some new input or direction, then these problems would be easier to solve or could potentially disappear altogether.

Working without a contract up front, and letting the energy mind choose the game to play, is **really** important and I think a 50/50 ratio of working with, and without contracts is the fair way to go, once you are an experienced player and visionary. For beginners, it is safe and soothing to work always with contracts, until you have found your own confidence.

The truth is that consciously, we really don't know what's going on; we don't have the full picture and there may be places and things we'd rather not look at, but if we did, that would make all the difference.

So that's when we say to the energy mind:

"Take me wherever you want me to go, give me whatever you want me to know..."

That can be scary at first, but it is also incredibly exciting and it opens new doors, brand new horizons and is probably the most wonderful way of playing the genius game that I know, personally speaking.

If you are playing with others, in therapy, as a game or in divination, the choice of going with a set up, or without and letting the energy mind/s choose where to go, remains the same.

For absolute beginners, and this applies much more to grown ups than it does to children who aren't full of fears of what they might discover in their energy minds if they took a good long look, using contracts is a nice safe way to give the feeling of control over the game.

Setting up some basic habitats, playing some nice games like just finding various healing environments, peace, tranquillity and beauty and having some fun sex, adventures and new discoveries to delight us and to replenish our starved systems to start with is the right way to go.

Every game will improve your understanding of how the energy mind works, how YOU WORK when you try to play as a complete human being who uses all their resources, probably for the first time ever. It also improves at the same time trust in the energy mind and its processes, and it removes fears.

It is perfectly OK to wait until you are really ready before moving on and working without contracts of any kind.

So Step 1 in the genius game is to make the contract and to say:

"Today, I want to..."

- play a friendly game
- learn something new about myself
- find help with problem X
- discover a new resource
- save an aspect
- save a lost soul
- get help for X
- do something magical
- explore a past life
- make contact with helpful spirits
- get closer to my soul
- help me sort out X
- count my blessings
- get something to make me smarter
- take the next step on my journey to enlightenment
- have fun with friends
- get the perfect habitat for healing, peace, relaxation, etc.
- go on a mission, journey, quest to X
- generate ideas for a new product
- find 23 new ways to save money
- remember powerfully motivational events from my life

- change my mind about X
- give me more energy for X
- ... ad infinitum!

Or simply say:

> ***"I want to play whatever game you bring to me today."***

Genius Symbol Warm Up Exercises

Tips On The Exercises

The warm up exercises are designed to get the flow of information from the energy mind to the conscious mind going.

They are really easy exercises that most people and children can do right away.

Here are some useful, global tips that can help you get good results pretty much right away.

1. **Watch your stress levels.**

   Stress breaks the flow of communication between the energy mind and the conscious mind. Simply taking a few deep breaths, moving your fingers, arms, shoulders, neck, spine, hips, knees, ankles, feet and toes to release locked up body stress is usually enough to calm you down so you can begin.

2. **While you play, watch your stress levels.**

   If you get angry or frustrated with yourself, take a few deep breaths and wriggle to release tension in the body, as above. Then you can go back to where you "lost the plot" by saying to yourself, "Where were we? What was the last thing we did?"

3. **Do these exercises quickly and don't dwell.**

   Don't furrow the brow, grit your teeth, bunch your fists or try to do any of this by pure will power - it doesn't work. If you really get nothing on a symbol, just put it aside for now and try another one. The first order of the day is to keep the flow and stay relaxed.

4. **Make the contract statements out aloud.**

   I usually advise to speak in your mind and in your voice at the same time and in chorus. Speaking out aloud is really helpful to get the flow going and to keep your mental focus on the symbols, keep that door open for the energy mind to respond.

5. **Hold the symbol in your hand...**

   ...and whilst looking with your eyes become aware of how it feels to the touch. "Listen" once you have said the contract as though you were literally waiting for the symbol to answer back. That creates the space for the information to come to you.

6. **If you lose concentration, simply go back to step 4 and the contract.**

   You can do this many times and you don't have to get annoyed, upset or angry. Think of it as hitting the reset button after a disturbance. Your focus will improve with practice.

7. **Comment on what you receive out aloud**.

   This really helps you keep your focus and get the flow of information going. It also tells your energy mind that you are listening and that you are paying attention.

8. **Thank your energy mind for any attempt at communication.**

   No matter what you receive, with the warm up exercises move along swiftly, say "Thank you!" out aloud for anything that you have received, put the symbol down and pick up the next one. Don't get involved or side tracked in the warm up exercises; they are only about practising the flow. You can do therapy or major problem solving in a little while.

9. **Always thank your energy mind at the end of the game.**

   When you are finished with the symbols, always thank your energy mind for its co-operation. Say it out aloud for all to hear, "Thank you, energy mind. That was really interesting. Looking forward to doing this again soon!" Good manners get you a long way, especially in intra-personal communications.

10. **Filter for your improvements after a session.**

    Regardless of how well you did during a first practice session, adopt an attitude of looking for the good in what you did. A single idea, a single flash vision or memory that surprised you is a good start and you can build on that. Be a good teacher to yourself, be really supportive and encouraging, and be patient. Rome wasn't built in a day and I assure you that getting better at receiving data streams from the energy mind is a whole lot quicker than even building a single story Roman villa, it's true!

I would also advise you to **start a journal** for your Genius Symbol exercises and write yourself a little report on each practice session.

You can use the journal to jot down ideas that occurred to you for future contracts, things that need to be investigated further, insights, important learnings and so forth.

As speaking out aloud helps with receiving, converting and understanding the data stream of the energy mind's communications, writing things down is also a whole body activity that helps make further connections in mind, body and spirit, and makes for a good record of your progress and improvements too.

Now, for some simple practice exercises.

The Memory Flash Exercises

Memory flash exercises are a great warm up to get images, sounds, tastes, scents and textures flowing in that rich stream of information that also produces stories and visions.

Steered through the contract, you can use memory flash exercises with The Genius Symbols for many purposes, from entertaining small children on a rainy afternoon, to improving your ability to access memories at will, to changing your mood, state and energy profoundly in minutes.

Memory flash exercises are really simple; pick a contract and get going!

Watch out for that moment when "thinking about it" becomes a flow of information; this usually happens three to seven symbols in with most people, and then, there is no stopping them.

Make a set up statement out aloud, pick up a symbol and let it trigger a memory. We call these memory **flashes** because the energy mind "flashes up" something quickly.

To develop a memory flash into a richer form of memory vision...

- ***...tell the story of the memory out aloud, even or especially if you are by yourself to engage your neurology;***
- ***...describe not just what you see, but also what you hear, scent, taste, feel and emote in the memory.***

You can have all the symbols face down and pick one at random, or have them face up and let one "jump out at you". When you are done with that symbol, put it aside and continue until all 23 have been done, or as many as you want to use on this occasion.

As a beginner, and while you are practising with The Genius Symbols, I would encourage you to **always go for the 23 symbols**, for the maximum flow, simply because it is so astonishing and feels so good to realise that our minds can do all these marvellous things, just for the asking!

"Give me a memory that will make me feel good today."

Pick a symbol, hold it in your hand/s, look at it and let a memory come to you.

Speak out aloud, tell a short story of that memory out aloud, and notice how that makes you feel.

When you have told the story, thank the symbol and put it aside.

Repeat the contract:

"Give me a memory that will make me feel good today."

... and repeat with the next symbol.

As you remember more and more good memories, you will start to feel better and better - about yourself, about your life, and you will notice a virtuous state spiral taking place.

This is a wonderful experience on many levels and very valuable indeed, so I commend this game to you especially.

You can play this game every day, and you will likely find that you get different memories flash up on different days. That is because you have so many memories, and your energy mind is sorting on what will make you feel good today - that is our old friend, the real time calculation, which makes energy mind communications so immensely appropriate, accurate and unique as well.

This is one of the truly extraordinary features of the human mind, and of course, we have so many memories to choose from, so you can be sure to get the perfect memories to make you feel good with this set up, ***every time.***

I'd like to make the comment that making you feel good might not always and only be about merry laughter; I have had occasions with this set up where I found very moving memories instead, but they did make me feel much better, even though some of them made me cry.

"Give me a memory that will help me do my best work today."

This is a more directive set up as you start work, and this will set you up amazingly to do whatever work you are going to do.

"Give me a forgotten memory I'll be glad to remember."

That's a super statement, quite wonderful, and really profound in its effects on a person. Please note we said "a memory I will be glad to remember" - like a lost treasure. If you don't put that into the set up statement, you are opening the door to remembering things that might not be so pleasant.

This can be used however in therapy and in self help to find something that needs working on by using a set up such as, "Give me a forgotten memory I need to remember."

"Give me a funny memory."

This is the perfect party game which can be played with anyone, and at any time. You don't need to teach the symbols, just have them be there and say, "Pick a symbol, hold it in your hand, look at the symbol and use it to remind you of a funny memory..."

I have actually used this at a truck stop with a bunch of lorry drivers who had never seen the symbols before, and it was brilliant – we laughed so much, it hurt in the end! There are many variations on this particular set up. "Give me a Monty Python sketch!" will produce for those who know many Monty Python sketches one each for each symbol quite reliably. Or you could play, "Give me a funny joke!"

Another variants a favourite story, a favourite movie, a favourite song, a favourite equation – these games definitely break the ice at parties, and they also break the ice inside if you are starting to learn the symbols and before making more profound symbol readings later on.

Pertinent Memory Exercises

Have you ever noticed that if someone tells you about their problems and asks you for advice, you are just full of it, and it really streams from you so easily?

And yet, when you are stuck yourself, you don't know what to do and no good ideas are coming to you?

The fact is that every person who has been alive for a few years on Earth and observed what goes on here has a lot of knowledge, learning, and wisdom accumulated inside, and it's often just a question of how to get it out into the open, so we can make use of it.

I once brought the Genius Symbols to a company which was run by a very experienced SEO who had been through all sorts of things in his business life, and it made no sense to me that he wouldn't know what to do. I guessed that he would have all the knowledge he needed to overcome the current crisis inside of him, but could not get it out because of stress, which blocks the energy mind communication channels. So I asked him to give me a memory on each symbol that was pertinent and relevant to the crisis at hand.

It was really amazing. He relayed such tremendously valuable information in the form of short memory stories, each one was good enough to be a chapter in a book called, "How to succeed in business."

Five symbols into it, and he gave a huge sigh and said, "My goodness, I had no idea only a few moments ago how much I actually know about all of this!"

It really was just stress that was blocking his knowledge, experience and wisdom, and the Genius Symbols got the flow of wisdom going again, and particularly delivered the practical answers to his problems now without a fail.

The Genius Symbols are a great way to get past the "I'm at my wits end... I've tried everything... and now I don't know what else to do..." stress block.

By showing you relevant or pertinent memories from your own life, it reconnects you with your own inner resources in a very profound way, and this is not just extremely stress relieving, but also good for your self esteem.

"Show me a memory that is good advice for this situation."

"Show me a memory that is pertinent to this situation."

"Show me a memory that is important to know in this situation."

"Remind me of something I already know that can help me now."

The 6 Senses Exercises

We have six senses which are present in normal waking reality, but they are also present "inside" - when we think, when we dream, when we remember, when we stream visions.

Every normal person has access to all of these senses, but what happens is that people specialise more in some than others, and thus become painters, musicians, cooks, football players, poets, or perfume makers respectively.

For full lucid visioning, as well as for full lucid living in general, of course **we want all six senses to be present at the same time** to give us the fullest and most complete "picture" of reality, with as much information in it as we can allow in through our senses.

We can practice our six senses by making a special contract that focuses on one of the senses.

> ***"Let me see something beautiful."***
> *This will ask for a picture, from the visual or seeing sense.*
>
> ***"Let me hear some beautiful sounds."***
> *This will ask for sound, from the auditory or hearing sense.*
>
> ***"Let me taste something beautiful."***
> *This will ask for taste, from the taste sense.*
>
> ***"Let me touch something beautiful."***
> *This will ask for a physical touch feeling, from the physical touch sense.*
>
> ***"Let me feel something beautiful."***
> *This will ask for a non-physical feeling, an emotion, from the emotion sense.*
>
> ***"Let me scent something beautiful."***
> *This will ask for a scent, from the scent or smell sense.*

I recommend when you start to practice the six senses separately.

Everyone finds some of them "easier" to start with than others; but none of them are any better than any of the others, it's just important that you should know which ones need more practice to really bring them online and make them as powerful and information rich as your favourites.

Also, don't try too hard. Simply make the statement, "I want to feel something beautiful," pick a symbol, and check out what happens next. Are you getting a feeling-memory? If you're not sure, just keep going, take the next symbol, and "listen" to the sense you are calling to your awareness.

It's amazing how quickly one gets better with practice doing this, and with more sensory information coming online, all your memories as well as all of your visions will become richer, deeper, more satisfying all around.

Improving Your Memory With The Genius Symbols

People often think that they have “a bad memory” or that they are not very good at remembering things. The problem lies not in the storage of memories, but in finding them again – being able to access memories. There is nothing “forgotten” in the human mind, it just gets mislabelled, misplaced, stress-blocked and it becomes unavailable.

Practising memory exercises with The Genius Symbols makes memories more available; and in the process of asking for memories on particular topics, and sorting them in that way, we get better at finding memories overall.

We get used to how it works that you ask for a memory, and then the memory is delivered to you by the energy mind.

This is a process of asking and then waiting for the answer. People get frantic and stressed and when they don't seem to get an answer right away, they do all sorts of things with their conscious mind when they should be silent for a moment and the answer would be given. This is why people wake up in the middle of the night with the answer to a quiz question that was given hours earlier; this is also related to thinking of what you should have said hours ago when it is way too late.

By practising this movement of asking for memories to be delivered, and then waiting for the answer to be given from the energy mind, we practice **the fundamental act of retrieving memories at will**.

This is extremely useful as I can happily attest to, and it extends to every form of learning, even very abstract learning such as formulae or computer code that needs to be remembered. Your energy mind can flash up the exact right code in front of you even if you have ever seen it only once when this system is fully operational.

To improve mental flexibility, and really improve internal communication and memory retrieval, playing the memory games with The Genius Symbols is an easy and delightful way to go. I really recommend this, you'll be delighted how memory games improve your mental functioning across the board with just a little basic practice.

Ideas Exercises

Do you have the TV show "The Apprentice" where you are in the world?

If you do, you will know how few good ideas a room full of people can barely manage and how sad it is that they don't have a single set of The Genius Symbols between them.

- **Generating ideas is something that should not be confined to the one time in your life when you really need a good idea.**

It's a skill, it's a flow, it's something we can learn to do, and it's natural to human beings.

The Genius Symbols can help us generate as many ideas as we want by engaging the infinite power of the energy mind to endlessly, and I mean ***endlessly***, generate new ideas.

Now the energy mind is who it is and it can't guarantee that they are all "good" ideas or that all ideas it produces should be acted upon.

That's for the conscious mind to decide later on; so it is important to understand that when we do these ideas exercises, we are literally just **generating a flow of ideas**.

In other words, don't stop and start judging the ideas at the time when you are generating ideas.

Think of it as apple picking. You are on the ladder, halfway up the tree, you are picking apples. That's it. Later on we can sort them into big and small apples, green and red ones, and take out the ones that have marks on them; for now, we're just picking apples.

Unconditionally, without judgement, without prejudice, accepting them all.

If you can do that, the world of ideas becomes infinite and you will never, ever have to struggle to find just one good idea, ever again, I promise!

The Gift Exercise

Think of a person you really like or even love, and make the following contract:

"Give me a wonderful gift for this person if I had all the money in the world."

Turn over one symbol at the time, get the idea flash up, and write down a short description or a title for the gift idea in your note book. Then move on immediately to the next symbol.

I have done this exercise quite often and on one occasion, wrote out the list of gifts and put them inside a birthday card. The person who received this was much moved.

If you want to be more practical and find a gift idea for a person that you can really give them, use a set up such as this:

"Give me a wonderful gift I can give to this person that will make them happy."

As before, write down all the ideas as they come, one per symbol, one after the other, until you have all 23 ideas written down.

Then choose one from the list as the one that will be given.

A more esoteric version of the Gift is The Fairy Gift. In fairy tales, fairy god mothers bestow qualities on babies, such as the gift of beauty, the gift of grace and the gift of courage.

"Give me a wonderful quality I can give to this person today."

On this occasion, rather than writing down the different qualities, hold out the symbol in your hand and say out aloud, "I send the gift of (beauty) to you!"

That is a lovely exercise that makes you feel good inside and in my mind can be more precious than buying an expensive gift for a person.

As energy forms don't cost anything and can be wonderfully varied and rich, you can send all kinds of The Gifts for all kinds of purposes, for example:

"Give me a healing gift for X tonight."

X can be anything you wish to send healing or positive energy to, including people, animals, a company, a project, a marriage, a city or a country, to mention but a few.

You can place a photograph or something that serves as a reminder in the centre, and then place all the symbols one by one around it in a circle, thus creating a symbol sphere.

This is a very powerful energy grid for distant healing and can also be used to charge physical objects[3] with additional energy, and to charge water.

---

3 For more esoteric/metaphysical uses of The Genius Symbols, please see Magic, Spells & Potions, DragonRising 2009.

23 Good Ideas For Anything Exercise

People think creativity is so difficult, but they really only think that because it is so rare they ask for even only one good idea, never mind 23.

Oh, if only I had just one good idea for...

- a new book
- a new movie
- a short story
- a new art project
- a new dish for the menu
- a new product
- a way to increase sales
- being more exciting in bed
- being a better father
- improving my house
- improving my personality
- saving money
- making money
- a new research direction
- solving this problem
- an invention that would change the world!

This sentence of, "Oh if only I had one good idea..." is a million miles away from saying, **"Give me 23 ideas right now!"** and expecting that this will be so.

With the energy mind it really is about getting what you ask for, every time.

But you do have to ask, and you do have to practice this a bit.

I would suggest to start with something that doesn't mean the world to you, that isn't your most stressful, most entrenched, most difficult problem and challenge in all the world.

Start with something that you don't normally worry too much about, or never worry about, to get the flow of ideas going, and to really feel, see, hear, experience for yourself how that works when ideas just flash up, immediately, instantly, without having to "think about it" or having steam coming out of your ears.

Try this exercise. It is easy, fun and will give you good practice how this works, so when you come to ask for 23 ideas for your own purposes, you will get a flow right away.

"Dear energy mind, give me an idea for a movie I would really like to watch."

Turn over one symbol at a time and let the idea come to you.

Make a quick note of the main idea on a notepad, then repeat the set up statement and pick the next symbol. Then simply continue on until you have all 23 movie ideas on your note pad.

This is to most people already quite astonishing. It gets even better when you do this again the following day and ask for another 23 ideas for movies that you would really like to watch.

You can follow this by 23 TV shows, and then another 23 TV shows, **and then another 23.**

If you don't like TV shows, do books, or articles, or the titles of poems, of concept albums, or new superheroes, or recipes for food that are completely original – just as long as you practice generating a stream of ideas, one after the other, on each occasion.

Creativity and ideas are endless. There comes a time when you do these exercises that you have a breakthrough – what we call a threshold shift – and you really understand that, it becomes a reality for you, you have proven to yourself that you can generate ideas at infinitum.

That's awesome, and as simple as it is, completely unheard of in the doings of humanity at this moment. It will give you a real competitive advantage, not just at work, either.

"Give me 23 good ideas to make my child happy," and "Give me 23 good ideas how to make my husband love me more," and "Give me 23 ideas how I can be a better Christian," is just the tip of the iceberg.

Being creative and having good ideas is **useful anywhere**, at any time, and always a really good idea when all is said and done, so it really is worth practising this.

Memory flashes and flash vision "ideas" exercises are great, and they have more than 101 uses in every day life.

However, if we want to change the world, we want to go beyond that, into a much deeper relationship with the energy mind.

We want to engage in a course of action that will teach us to understand how the energy mind works, how it communicates, and how it can give us access to information that no human being has ever talked about or written about before.

This is where we go from having good ideas to actually becoming a genius by any other name - someone who can stream real visions like the world has never seen, and create absolutely unique systems, solutions, works of art that are truly inspired.

Now we are ready to play the game in space and time!

A Very First Sanctuary

If you have never played Project Sanctuary before, or if you are playing with someone who has not, teaching it to someone, playing with a child or introducing Project Sanctuary to groups, a "First Sanctuary" is a good way into the amazing worlds of Project Sanctuary that is easy and gentle.

There are no stories to play here to start with; just a perfect place to explore and become familiar with, and to have time to adjust to the magic of Sanctuary and how things work.

The "First Sanctuary" is simply a habitat with a very nice house, and all is designed to be as wonderful, exciting, comfortable and delightful as the player themselves can allow it to be for now.

Pick out the symbols for space, time, weather, land, plants, and house and put them out in a line in front of you or your playing partner.

Place your finger on the space symbols and tell your energy mind what you want to do, make the contract for the game.

On this occasion it would be something like this:

"Take me to a perfect place in space and time, a Sanctuary of my very own, a beautiful place that is just right for me to be happy!"

Choose your own words to express this sentiment, please do!

Now, place your finger on the time symbol and ask yourself, "What is the perfect time of day for me? The perfect time of year?"

With that established, we move on to "What is the perfect weather?"

Then, "What is the landscape?" and "What kind of plants are here, what is the vegetation like?"

Finally, for the First Sanctuary, place your finger on the house symbol and ask for the perfect house or home or dwelling for you at this time.

Now, you have a Sanctuary of your very own which you can explore, add things to, try to make some changes in, or simply move in and relax and enjoy.

Even in a First Sanctuary, there are many things to be discovered; this is a wonderful process and you come out of it with a real place in space and time you can visit at any time you like – your first outpost in the amazing worlds of Sanctuary.

Note:

In the olden days of New Age ideas and techniques, people only used to have ***one*** *Sanctuary.*

Project Sanctuary is much more fluid than that, and much richer.

You can have as many Sanctuaries as you like, and you can make a new one each time you want to – it costs nothing, it is extremely educational at the multi-level, and it's great practice for you as well.

You have to remember that **our needs change ALL THE TIME** – from day to day, from moment to moment, and never mind from year to year, or decade to decade!

Sometimes we overheat and need cooling in a winter world; sometimes we are parched and need a tropical downpour in a rain garden. Sometimes we're swamped and a stay in a golden desert is just what the spirit doctor ordered on this occasion.

It goes on and on. Sometimes we need to be quiet and alone, and at other times, what we really need is a big festival with lots of people, lots of coloured lights and lots of activity and celebration to put us "right".

Every person has a huge range of needs for energies that change every day and so to have many different Sanctuaries to choose from is perfect and as it should be.

I often think of this as most people not having a holiday home at all they can visit for fun and relaxation; and even fewer people have lots of holiday homes they can visit as and when the seasons change so they are always **in the perfect place at the right time**.

In Sanctuary, you're one of those super-rich people who can "jet off" for a night out in Paris or a dip on a tropical beach or a bit of skiing in the snowy mountains at will and any time you feel like it.

Indeed, and what with alien space travel, dimensional travel and time travel too, your choices are infinitely more and more appealing than what's on offer to the richest man on Earth!

So don't get stuck in a single Sanctuary, no matter how wonderful it may be – let go, be playful and create MANY in response to your ever changing moods, needs, desires and wants.

It is the healthy thing to do!

The Classic Game

First Sanctuary style habitats for rest and relaxation are one thing, but once we have rested and relaxed, it's time to really play the game in space and time.

This involves action, often high drama, challenges, and the most fascinating stories imaginable.

It is also so that people who think they need eternal peace and rest because they are so worn out will find that actually, the activity and interest of the real Project Sanctuary game stimulates them, charges them up and gives them much more energy than just endlessly lying on perfect beaches with a dream lover ever could.

Then of course, there are those magical and priceless threshold shifts beckoning, just waiting for you beyond the horizon...

So, are you ready for a real adventure?

Find the seven symbols for space, time, weather, landscape, plants, friend and artefact.

These are the key ingredients to start a Project Sanctuary vision of your very own; something that is completely unique to you and that is created for you and by you with the help of your energy mind, which of course is also "you."

Have the seven symbols ready to hand and place the first symbol, space, in front of you to start our famous game in space and time.

Know why you are seeking this experience - think about the contract, our set up, what you are looking for, what problem you want solved, what kind of habitat you're looking for, who you want to play for etc.

Formulate the contract, agreement or set up in our mind so it is ready to go to start the game.

Now:

Place the space symbol in front of you. Put your finger or just your attention on the space symbol. Take a deep breath and if you want to, see the universal sandbox, the starry space in which we play, although that isn't necessary to make it work. Make your contract now and speak it out aloud.

Place the time symbol next and ask yourself - "What is the time of day?" Get a sense of that, and then "What is the time of year?" to get a sense of that also. Even if time is irrelevant, you are on an alien planet or in a different dimension, we have an internal time clock which will give us the first reference points.

Place the weather symbol and ask yourself, "What is the weather?" This will give you information about many things, and a lot of them are not visual but sensory impressions of hot and cold, wind, sunlight on your skin and so forth. If you are indoors, think what is the atmosphere here to give you a sense of the weather inside this room or building. As the weather affects everything else in the environment, this starts to make the habitat real.

Place the land symbol and ask yourself, "What is the landscape? What is this land?" Take your time and turn around 360° to see the land that surrounds you. Physically pointing at special features such as, "There is the mountain," or, "There is the lake!" can be very helpful to get your bearings and information about what's there.

Place the plant symbol and ask yourself, "What vegetation exists here?" or, "What kind of plant kingdom exists here?" Habitats don't always have plants that we readily recognise but there is merit in tuning into the land and becoming aware of what plant life there is - even if there is only microscopic life, that will be very relevant.

Now take a moment to familiarise yourself with this habitat. Walk around, look at things, look down at the ground, touch things, feel things, smell the air, and pay attention to how it FEELS being here.

The basic habitat is the most important key to all that comes afterwards; there is much merit in exploring a little, finding your bearings, and letting the information about this unique habitat stream into you from all levels, and in all ways.

Place the friend symbol and ask for a friend to come forward. If you have played before, you will have one or more good friends you are already familiar with; but it is also possible that a new friend who is particularly well placed to help you with this unique game can come forward. Take a moment to familiarise yourself with the friend should they be new.

Finally, place the artefact symbol to set the game in motion. The artefact will guide you towards what you need to do in this habitat to gain what you were looking for in your original contract or set up. All that remains to do now is to play the game as it unfolds.

Using The Symbols Inside The Game

It has been my experience that once you've got the vision going with the Classic Game as described above, it takes on a life of its own and simply proceeds from one thing to the next in a very natural fashion, all the way to the threshold shift.

We do have 23 symbols overall however and these can certainly add a few extra dimensions to the game.

You can use all the symbols inside the game as follows.

- Play the story as it happens and when you come to a blockage or a place where things seem to get hairy, use extra symbols to help you overcome the problem.
- Place the rest of the symbols face down and draw random symbols to help shape the story all the way through.
- Place the rest of the symbols face up and let your attention be guided to certain symbols that help with the unfolding story and move it along.
- Choose a particular symbol consciously to help you make progress.

Remember that any story, vision or sequence of events **needs to move forward towards its threshold shift.**

Usually, we ask, "What happens next?" should there be a block in the story or it doesn't seem to go anywhere. This is always helpful, and drawing more symbols until the story resolves itself to the threshold shift in the end is easy and very helpful.

> *Note:*
>
> *Even if a story runs straight from the classic game to the threshold shift instantly and without a hitch, sometimes it is really nice to go through all the symbols as well afterwards and observe the influences "behind the scenes".*

Applying all 23 symbols to any single vision, story, memory or event gives you a truly astonishing richness of understanding and insight and creates all together, a most remarkable multi-level learning experience.

An Example Of The Classic Game

Using my beach pebbles with the symbols drawn on them in metallic marker, I set out to play a game I can use for an example in this manual and that would also help me get to the next level with my own unfoldments.

So that was my set up and contract on the space symbol.

Here is what happened next.

> *The time is mid afternoon. It is sunny but also very windy, bright sea winds, warm and wonderful. The landscape is a tropical island, close to the beach is where I'm standing, very beautiful. The land slopes down towards the sea and there are many shrubs and bushes of rich, rich green and many bear exotic blossoms. In the distance, I can see tropical trees, palm trees.*
>
> *I am standing on the beach, soft white sand, very warm under my bare feet, and the ocean is to my left. A friend is approaching, a friendly dark skinned Shaman I have met before, and I greet him happily. He takes me to the water's edge, where I find a really amazing deep sea shell with many turns, green blue on the outside and iridescent pink on the inside.*
>
> *As I pick it up I realise that this is a magic shell which will call to beings that live beneath the sea if I was to pick it up and blow into it...*

As you can see/feel, all the components for a truly amazing Sanctuary experience are right there, ready to go. This is also a puzzle, of course – why am I being given this shell? What lies beneath the sea which wishes to communicate with me and has, to all intents and purposes, provided me with their own version of a mobile phone?

When you get to this point in your own story, in your own habitat, with your own friend/s, and an artefact that was delivered straight from your energy mind, you will feel a true sense of excitement, and sometimes also a little fear.

What will we discover?

We don't know.

But that's exactly the beauty of Project Sanctuary, and it's exactly why it is so exciting to the right people, and especially to those who really want evolution, who really want to find out how much more there is to themselves than they thought or feared there was.

Now it's time to be courageous.

If you need any extra resources before you can start to play the game for real, you can now draw further symbols, as many as you need; or you can simply get started without further ado because in truth, you are magic incarnate here and you have all the powers of time and space at your command – you just need to remember that **"This is all made from energy, this is only energy!"**

Note:

If you are playing with another and it is their story, encourage them to go forward and remind them of their ability to do magic in these realms of pure energy data.

If they are really scared and hesitant, ask them to pick up the magic symbol, look at it and ask for a special magic skill, or tool, or any form of magic help that is going to be useful here to come forward.

Keep the magic symbol close by as you go through the story; it will help you overcome sticking points, moments of doubt or fear and keeps the momentum of the story, which is very important.

In my example, I noticed a hesitation – I didn't really want to blow into the shell, although I very much wanted to hear what it sounded like and knew it was the right thing to do, and also, that nothing bad could happen that I couldn't deal with.

So I looked at the magic symbol and as I did, a ship sprang into being – a beautiful very old sailing ship with square sails but it was magical in every way. I went on board right away with my friend the Shaman, and felt much better as the ship sailed out into the ocean, because I would be meeting those I was about to call half way. That was much better, much more correct.

Now, I couldn't wait to reach that special place in the deep oceans – standing at the bow of the ship as it elegantly drove forward into the emerald green waves was amazing all by itself...

Important!

Once a vision has become revealed, you need to take the time to play it through to a threshold shift.

All the benefits and amazing results ONLY come from playing the story all the way to its resolution!

As you can see, you can play the story from here without involving any further symbols; but you can also use further symbols to deepen and refine the unfolding process.

There are three ways to go on from here.

1. Now pick any symbol and let a connection to the story come to you whilst you look at it. You can repeat this with one or all of the remaining symbols, and you can even do it more than once and keep returning the symbol you've drawn back into the reservoir, so you can draw "Angels" three times if that's how long it takes for you to get the message. ☺

2. You can look at the rest of the symbols in this order and ask yourself, "Is this helpful/relevant to the story?" The fact is that there are always plants around, always animals, crystals make up a vast percentage of the Earth's crust, everything is full of spirits – but in this particular case, is that symbol relevant and or helpful to the unfoldments of the story? Usually you get a clear cut sense of either no, or yes and that's because... (insert idea, understanding, connection etc. that helps the story). Should you go blank, put the symbol away and come back to it later. It might be important but its time has not yet come.

3. You can leave the rest of the symbols and just continue the story; when you need extra help, take a look if something jumps out at you that holds the key to the next step in the story.

In this example story, the one about the shell, the shaman and the magic boat, a truly awesome vision unfolded for me that involved beings living deep, deep below the oceans in an astonishing kingdom of lightness and light; it's a long story, it's my story, but I am most grateful to have experienced it.

My energy mind sent me this vision to help me change something important for me, help me discover something amazing that I never knew was even there, and together we made a re-connection that was deep and profound – the threshold shift.

➢ **These visions, stories and adventures are priceless.**

It is my deepest wish that you too will discover this for yourself, receive your own visions and play your own stories, in your own time – it is such an enriching experience, it really does change who you think you are at the end of the day in a most profound and structural way.

A Personalised Layout

Instead of starting with the usual run of the symbols from the classic game, you can spread out the symbols and choose where you want to start.

Let a symbol draw your attention, and start right there. Pick it up and place it somewhere else as you let the story unfold.

> <u>*An important note:*</u>
>
> *The faster you can work with this, the better your results will be. Please remember that even the conscious mind already works at light speed, and the energy mind just laughs at that and calls light speed a snail's pace! Ideas can flash faster than lightning if you let them, and half the reason why intelligent people have such trouble with meditation is that it's all waaaaay too slooooow and everyone gets bored before we've even started!*
>
> *By yourself, with children and at parties, you can just pick symbols and have everyone shout out things that come to mind – instant entrance into a whole infinity of topics, of memories, of events, of ideas just streaming forth freely – if you let them.*

Genius Symbol Patterns In Brief

There are many different ways to use the Genius Symbols to start a conversation or a communication with your energy mind.

The Classic Game

The first and most globally useful as well as the most profound use of the Genius Symbols is The Classic Game, which we have already learned. This is the original Game In Space & Time which creates a stable habitat in which you play out a Project Sanctuary story through to the threshold shift.

The Classic Game is unbeatable as a device to teach you genius level, systemic thinking, metaphor, the laws of the energy mind, and much about the world at large, so hold a special place in your heart and in your head for the Classic Game, and play this in preference as well when all else fails.

The information you get from the Classic Game is of a different order than all other games and it never ceases to amaze how the Classic Game goes way beyond the questions that were asked, and so often, if not always, shows us how limited in many ways our questions really are.

Single Symbol Flash Visions

Here, you deal with one symbol at a time and ask the same question or make the same contract on each symbol.

The quickest and easiest way to work with single symbol flash visions is to have all the symbols face up, state the contract, and note which symbol jumps out at you.

Pick it up, hold it in your hand and re-state the contract out aloud if necessary to get the insight or flash vision this symbol has triggered.

You can repeat this with as few or as many symbols as you like.

All 23 Symbols Flash Visions

Have all the symbols face down, or in a bag or box so you can pick one at random and ask the same question/state the same contract to all 23 symbols, one at a time.

This gives you a hugely powerful Venn diagram on your problem or request, and it really stretches your conscious mind.

You might think that querying all 23 symbols is a lot of hard work but it is really worth it. If we are left to our own devices, we only ever end up picking the easy symbols or the obvious ones. By really thinking and engaging each one, this really expands the mind. Also, doing 23 symbols often causes a threshold breach and you will find ideas start not just flowing, but cascading at high speed. Indeed, we call this "a cascade" and it happens when you push past the point where you "think" you can't consciously think of anything else.

Especially for beginners, I highly recommend using all 23 symbols for single symbol queries as often as possible. It's extremely interesting, very educational and will speed up your path towards more and more genius ideas.

The Symbol Sphere

It is natural to place the symbols in a circle, especially when working with the whole set and single symbol flash visions.

You will find that when all are done, all the symbols have spoken, if you will, and they are all in a circle, something interesting and strange happens – the entirety of the information becomes more than the sum of its parts and the symbol sphere is born.

For people who work with energy, symbol spheres can be extremely powerful tools and turn the Genius Symbols into a "magic machine" with a thousand and one uses.

Beginners too can use the combined power of all the symbols in the symbol sphere by starting with a contract that may be written down on a piece of paper, may be an image of a person, a symbol of a company, or an actual object of some kind that is either being queried or charged, that is placed in the center, with all the symbols facing down around the outside. One by one, the symbols are turned over and activated.

An easy example is a Blessing symbol sphere, whereby a picture of a person is placed in the center, and on each symbol, a relevant blessing is created; when all 23 blessings have been given, the entire symbol sphere becomes one blessing that is more than the sum of its parts for that person in the center.

Symbol spheres also lend themselves to more than one person taking turns and adding their input to the topic; this is very useful for generating ideas for group projects in a company, department, or family.

Genius Symbol Patterns

As you can imagine, with 23 symbols the number of patterns you can make are endless; plus you can replicate any divination pattern that can be done with runes, tarot cards, numbers and letters with the Genius Symbols too and achieve remarkable results.

Three symbol readings can include one symbol each for past, present and future; for plus, minus and interesting; for you, me and them; above, here, and below; and so on and so forth.

You can use 12 symbols for the houses of the Zodiac and create astrology based readings; and combinations of three, five and seven symbols to create instant stories, complex ideas and poetry.

Using A Pendulum

Place all the symbols in a circle, pattern, grid or in any order and use a pendulum to have you choose 1, 3, 6, 9 or the order of all of them for you to read as a separate exercise.

You can have them facing up, or down.

Now we have all the basics we need to really use The Genius Symbols to activate our natural, inborn genius, and using our genius, which is both of our minds working together and in harmony, to make our lives better, and the world a better place to be for all humanity.

As the Genius Symbols are entirely content free and all they do is to generate genius visions, answers and ideas, they can be used in every context of human endeavour; anywhere and at any time a person or a group of people might inspiration, creativity, imagination, a good idea, a new idea, a different answer, a new way forward, a new story or simply something wonderful to do with their wonderful minds.

In the next section, we are going to look at some of the infinite applications for the Genius Symbols and the people who play with them.

Games To Play With The Genius Symbols

In this section, we are going to discuss and discover different ways in which you can make playing with the Genius Symbols work for you.

Don't be fooled by the word "game".

Yes, it is play in absolute essence as we discover new things and go where our attention and fascination is going to lead us.

Yes, we are playing a game.

And yes, this can be as deadly serious as it needs to be.

You can play for your life.

I always do because what I learn here, the visions and the threshold shifts shape my life and my understanding of life.

Just because something is serious, however, does NOT need to mean that you have to approach it in a dour and miserable way.

- **There is a world of difference between being respectful, and being terrified.**

When we are afraid or stressed, the light goes out. Everything becomes heavy and scary and uncontrollable and too hard, too difficult.

We literally lose contact with the high, fine, fast, flowing, delightful realms of true creation and fall into rock hard dungeons of our own making.

Every one of us has the propensity to fall into that, depending on the topic at hand; that is what we call ***magic failure***, probably just a simple, structural energy reversal that we have on certain topics and at certain moments under high stress.

Please watch yourself for when this happens; when you no longer understand that we are playing a game, and when you lose perspective.

Please know that everyone, and that includes me, has topics where they lose the plot and everything becomes hard and dark all of a sudden, "deadly serious" and it seems that this one thing, this one problem, this one challenge is different from all the others, that it is somehow exempt from the universal laws that rule **everything.**

Please also know that the more you play in Sanctuary, and especially if you follow the 50/50 rule of balancing your serious quests and driven intentions to be a "better" this and that with rest, relaxation, fun and pure joy, the easier it will become to play every topic with delight.

To your best to remember to stay light, light on your feet, light in your mind, light in your heart, clear, focused, and with a positive intention. That is the state from which genius solutions to your problems will appear, and it is the only state that helps them appear.

Remember that whatever game you play, you are playing for a full resolution of the problem.

- **At the end, there is the threshold shift.**

The light at the end of the tunnel, if you will.

THERE IS ALWAYS A LIGHT.

Sometimes we can't see it right away, and we doubt the very fact that it is really there; but as I've said, the more you play, the more certain you will become that there is a light, a threshold shift, and that **you** can find it; when that happens, you can call yourself a true Project Sanctuary player and a visionary genius, at that.

As you read through the ideas and examples as to what kind of games you can play with the Genius Symbols, start to pay attention to how you react and respond to the games that are suggested here.

For example, the very first section is headed "Therapy Games".

Does that make your toes curl? Do you go into instant rejection at the thought of any kind of "therapy"? I don't blame you if you do, indeed I don't, but come on, I think you and I both know that there isn't a person on Earth who could do with some form of therapy, some form of resolving something from the past that is holding them back in their lives today.

Likewise, if the only reason you bought this book is because you're convinced that "therapy is the answer!" and you are completely attracted by the therapy games alone, I would also and likewise, ask you to think again and widen the horizons a little.

I would put it to you that every one of these sections and their various games has something to offer to everyone, somewhere along the line.

If you find out which games you like to play more than others, and simply make a mental note for now that this is so, you will have learned something very important about yourself already – and before even having your first proper vision, at that.

So I would ask you sincerely to give all the sections your best attention, and including the "games for children".

Just because you don't have any children, or you don't have any around you any more, doesn't mean that you couldn't have some fun and some extremely interesting insights if you were to play those games with "your child within" instead.

Indeed, being able to remember what it was like to play as a child would, with that total focus and unconditional fascination about the world and everything in it, soaking up the world like a sponge, that is an ability that we seek to recover when we "play the greatest game on Earth" - the game in space and time, the one true game of the human mind set free from all limitations of the hard, and all the universe at its command.

Playing with the symbols and your own aspects is a very interesting and multi-dimensional experience.

With that said, received and understood, here are some examples of how to play with the Genius Symbols for threshold shifts, insights, breakthroughs, learnings, wisdom and evolution as the prizes which await those who will play the game.

Therapy Games

To remind us briefly, therapy means healing.

I personally mean for healing to mean this:

"To put to rights what once went wrong."

> Note:
>
> *No miracles of physical healing are promised here. Project Sanctuary deals with* ***mind, energy, intelligence and emotion.*** *Even though all these are essential to physical health, any effects on physical health are considered side effects, welcome though they may be.*

With Project Sanctuary and the Genius Symbols, you can think of therapy as a game, played by one or more people, to get threshold shifts that will lead them forward on their own personal path to healing.

Project Sanctuary is all about resolution and harmonic evolution; putting things in their rightful places, bringing connection and nourishment to systems that are shown to us by the energy mind. In essence, all Project Sanctuary games we play is a form of therapy in that sense.

However, it is the contract you make before you start to play which decides the direction and the purpose of the game.

- **An important note: Project Sanctuary treats the events in memories, false memories, dreams, fantasies, and Project Sanctuary stories EXACTLY THE SAME.**

All these are nothing but intrapersonal data and therefore underlie the basic principles, and all can be **evolved** towards a new level of functioning - and then they can be evolved more and further towards yet another higher level, and so on.

For some systems, this new level of functioning can mean that they start to function for the first time; for some it means an improvement in how well they are allowed to function.

We do not seek instant perfection but instead, ongoing evolution which will lead eventually to the best we can be, whatever that may turn out to mean in the end.

From Events Psychology, we have inherited the slogan,

"You don't have to solve it, only evolve it!"

It is important to remember, especially in the case of "real memories", that these events that once were, only now exist in the neurology – memories are energetic data. So are dreams, stories, things you were told, visions you may have had or nightmares – it is all data, all energy.

It isn't just all energy – **<u>it is also now ONLY energy.</u>**

It's only energy data - and energy data can be changed. We can step into the data stream as we do and make changes there at will. Then, what once was one thing, becomes another story altogether; and if we get our story straight, it will lead to a much, much happier life for all concerned.

I must mention this one more time because it is central to the healing applications of Sanctuary – we do NOT differentiate between a dream, a memory, a false memory, or a story.

- **It's all data, it's only data – it is only energy.**

Now when you change a "real" memory using Project Sanctuary, you don't "lose" it, because the change itself becomes a part of the memory – **you remember that you changed the memory.**

This has an important threefold effect.

- Firstly, when we change a memory using Project Sanctuary it becomes resolved; it is no longer painful, damaging or dangerous to the system; the toxicity has been removed – **the memory has evolved**.
- Secondly, as we remember that we changed the memory, the original events still exist, they are still on record just as they once were so nothing was lost, but a new forward momentum has been gained as well.

- Thirdly, as we have actively **connected** the memory from then to now and evolved it, it has become available as a resource and is now a system that functions towards our highest outcomes.

People very rightfully do not want to lose their memories or deny them because all your memories and all your visions and fantasies together, **are your life**; and it is important that you should know so can tell others when you work with them that you get to keep the story intact – but it doesn't end there, the story continues beyond that time or trauma into a resolution which we can achieve today.

What all of that means is that you can "call" a specific event, an energy form of any kind, using the symbols and a contract.

For example,

"Take me to a place in time and space where an aspect still needs help."

This aspect, or past self, will experience the current you as their friend who has come to aid them in their moment of need. The energy mind gets to choose the aspect that needs your help the most at this time.

You can be more specific and say in your contract:

"Take me to an aspect which, if I helped it evolve today, would have the greatest benefits in solving my current problems with X."

Once you have arrived in the habitat, and you have an idea of what is going on there, you can draw further symbols to evolve the story and move it into a different direction.

Please Note:

Do remember that you have mastery of time in Sanctuary. You can choose where to intervene and change the past, if you want to think of it like that. Generally, the aspect in that particular time and place that is shown to you by your energy mind is what needs your help right there and then.

The contracts allow you to be as specific, or as global, as you need to be on any given occasion.

Remember there is more to healing than just trauma clearance, although that is often the first thing which needs to be done to bring more lucidity and peace to the whole system.

The contract, "Take me to an aspect that didn't get what it needed," for example, will allow you to bring nourishment and energy into systems that might need this still and are not functioning because they never got the right nutrients, as it were.

- **Think of health in the widest metaphorical sense, and likewise of health and healing through therapy.**

There are many ways in which we can help ourselves and others by addressing aspects who have played an important part in the formation of our personalities and our beliefs about the world.

One particular thing I would like to mention here are Guiding Stars[4], moments of extreme joy and possibly even transcendental happiness which can also cause major problems because they were "too good to be true" and aspects can get stuck there just the same as they can get stuck in a high trauma memory habitat.

For example, a first love may be so overwhelming that a person at the time made a vow that "I shall never love anyone else as long as I live!" in a moment of high emotion.

---

4 Guiding Stars are an important part of Events Psychology. See Events Psychology, Dr S Hartmann, DragonRising Publishing 2009.

To go to such an aspect and gently ask it to rephrase that statement into something more ecological, such as, "I really love this person with all my heart! I can love!" can really bring wonderful forward movement into stuck and entrenched systems.

Guiding Stars play an extremely important part in addictions, fetishes, philias of all kinds as well as being responsible for all manner of disturbing life patterns and also play a crucial part in the formation of beliefs, values and attitudes so they should not be overlooked. Evolving Guiding Stars has more inherent potential for major life changes than evolving trauma memories and is currently not being dealt with sufficiently in standard psychology.

A set up of, "Take me to a time and place where there is a Guiding Star that limits me today!" can take you to such places; and if your energy mind shows you to a habitat, please take this to mean that you are now really supposed to change what you find there – no matter if it seems wonderful already on the surface.

A Therapy Game Example

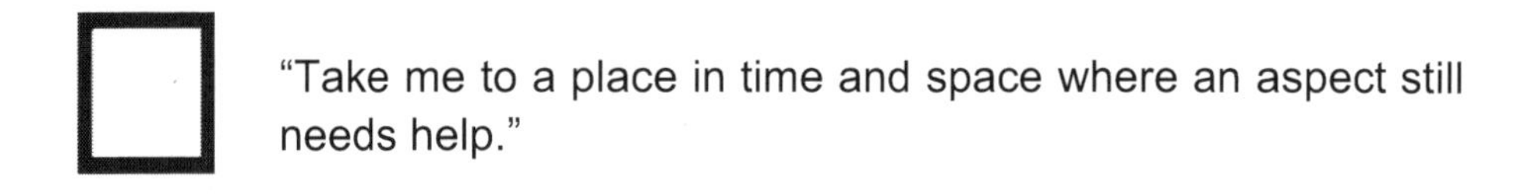

"Take me to a place in time and space where an aspect still needs help."

What is the time of day? The time of year?

"It is mid morning. Autumn, cold and clammy."

What is the weather?

"Misty, cold, very cold. Everything is wet and there is a wet cold wind blowing. I'm very cold."

What is the land?

"I'm on a sea shore, the tide is out, all there is is a huge long stretch of wet cold sand, dirty looking, all the way out to the horizon."

Do you know now where this is, when this is, what this is about? Do you recognise the memory?

"I recognise the memory. I was sent to a boarding school by the sea when I was 6 years old. It was a terrible place and I got ill so I'm told and had to be sent back home. I don't remember anything about it. Well, I do now. I remember the endless marches in the freezing cold. And being constantly hungry and tired. And nobody cared. I don't even think anyone there even knew me by name."

Pick a symbol to evolve the memory and save the aspect on the sea shore.

"I choose the Friend. I needed a friend. Someone to look out for me, someone to be friendly."

And what happens next?

"A friendly looking man with a scarf wrapped around his neck comes over to me. He smiles at me, notices how cold I am.

"I am so relieved that someone has finally noticed there is something wrong with me..."

What else can we do to make the aspect feel better?

"He takes his scarf off and puts it around my neck. It is warm and woolly, it really makes me feel so much better. I feel a great sense of relief, like I'm not going to die of the cold now. Not even the hunger is so bad any more..."

What happens next?

"I go back to the school with the other children and we get something to eat at last. Everything is going to be alright, I'm going to survive this, after all."

How do you feel now?

"I feel very calm. When the friendly man put the scarf around my neck in the story, it was like a weight lifted from me - here, now - and I felt warm and saved all of a sudden. I still feel warm, and strong.

> "I did survive it, and the poor aspect isn't walking around on that unforgiving freezing shore any longer, thinking it was going to die."

As you can see from this example, evolving a memory is easy once you have found the "habitat" - the place in time and space where that person's former self or aspect got stuck and thought they were going to die.

The energy mind provided the solution - the friendly man with his scarf. It is important to note that both the friendly man as well as the scarf are both energy constructs, things made of energy, energy cocktails if you will that were designed to be the exact right antidote to the state of the poor aspect. And the "real time" feelings of relief and warmth in the body tell us that this wasn't just a mental exercise, but a real form of time healing for this person in question.

Healing Games

The Universe is full of healing energies – so many places to go to get healing.

Healing stories are central to playing Project Sanctuary but you can also simply draw a "daily symbol" and turn to that realm for the healing energies of the day.

Spend a short time meditating on how this symbol can help you heal if you open yourself to those energy forms; a vision often unfolds from that as do amazing threshold shifts that can change your life.

Through experience, we have found that **sleep habitats,** places where you go when you are lying in bed and before you go to sleep, can be very powerfully helpful when you are seeking healing.

Just before you go to bed, ask for a habitat that would be just perfect for you to go to tonight, where you can rest and soak up powerful healing energies that will help you on every level.

Note:

Don't get stuck in one habitat, no matter how beautiful it is or how much better it makes you feel.

Ask every time afresh, at least for a week or a month. If the original habitat is still the right one, it will come back automatically; but often this changes from day to day, especially as your healing journey progresses and new and other energies are needed.

Another version of using healing habitats are the instant healing habitats.

At any time of day, you can ask yourself, "What would be the perfect place in time and space for me to connect with, right now?"

With just a little practice, a habitat will flash into your mind and by tuning into the energies of that if only for a moment, you will find that your stress goes down, and as if you had just taken some vitamins, or drunk a healthy fruit juice – a wonderful experience, freely available at any time.

You can use a symbol sphere to send distant healing to another person, company, animal, landscape, the whole world; and you can use that also for yourself, tuning in on the different gifts from every symbol one at a time, culminating in the entire symbol sphere at the end which is always more than the sum of its parts. You can also use a symbol sphere to charge water with that 23fold, 23vibration, custom made healing intention you have created whilst working with the symbols.

If you remember, you can pitch your contracts to get very practical, very down-to-earth indeed.

You can ask for practical advice on how to manage or evolve an illness forward towards health better and you will get 23 useful answers that can do a lot to get you better sooner in mind, body and spirit.

Past Life Regression

Many people do PLR for therapy, but it also an amazing game in its own right to find out more about your motivations in this life, to answer questions you have about yourself, and give you a bigger picture perspective on what's happening in this life, here and now.

Past Life Regression is endlessly fascinating, and if you play it simply as a Genius Symbol game and don't put on it any form of religious conviction or make a huge deal out of it, can teach you reams about yourself. In that way, it can also be played by just about anyone, and thoroughly enjoyed on all levels.

"Show me to a past life that, if we resolve it today, will make all the difference to X."

"Show me to a past life that will help me understand my soul better."

"Take me to a past life that will help me understand my own strengths better."

"Take me to a past life to help me discover important resources I didn't even know I had!"

"Take me to a past life that was amazing, and wonderful!"

These and many other contracts using the Classic Game will bring you just fantastic experiences that will really help you understand yourself and others better, and make you wiser, too.

Soul Pilot

Becoming a Soul Pilot[5] is a particularly fascinating aspect of Project Sanctuary – instead of doing the "poor me!" endless therapy games and hunting for yet more injured aspects of the self, we actually offer our services to help others; we go into Sanctuary to find lost souls who need someone just like we are, a living person, to help free them because they are stuck between the planes of existence.

The lost souls, like all things, need to evolve – they are stuck and we help them move on their own rightful path.

For any person who steps up to be a PS Soul Pilot, exactly the right types of lost souls that are a perfect vibrational match will come forward.

This means that no matter how forsaken or damaged you are personally, you will be the perfect match for some of the many lost souls out there – and for some of them, you may indeed be, the only hope they have for rescue.

In Soul Piloting, we are shown to a time and place where there is someone who needs our help. This can be quite challenging but is also immensely satisfying – keep your Magic symbol close by and remember you have Friends and many other resources to help you help that other.

"Show me to a lost soul who needs my help today."

---

[5] For more information about Soul Pilot work, please see www.SoulPilots.com

Meetings

As we are human, we learn the most from other humans and from interacting with others in general. It doesn't matter if these others are angels, spirits, dead ancestors, guides, more evolved souls who offer their astral services to us in a Soul Piloting kind of way, animals, aliens – there are worlds upon worlds of beings "out there" who would help us grow, evolve and develop if we were to meet with them, and interact with them.

"Take me to the perfect place in time and space where I can meet with someone who can help me with X."

With that contract in conjunction with the Classic Game, you will go somewhere and indeed, meet someone for you to interact with, and to learn from.

"Take me to the perfect place in time and space to meet my mother."

That set up creates a habitat which will be safe for you to meet a living or dead person who you want to talk to in order to come to a resolution or forward movement with that person.

The landscapes, weathers, vegetations and all parts of the habitats are incredibly important to provide "the right setting" for these types of meetings, to help you feel safe and to make it so that the meeting has every chance of succeeding.

"Take me to the perfect place in time and space where I can meet with Jesus."

"Take me to the perfect place in time and space where I can meet a representative of my own soul."

"Take me to the perfect place in time and space where I can meet someone who will teach me about physics."

The choices of games, and the possibilities of interactions and learning are truly limitless.

Block Removal

One of the crazy things about us human beings is that we are often the last to know what's wrong with us or where our blockages truly lie to get what we want out of life.

We're so used to living inside of our own problems, it's like fish with water.

Our energy mind can really help us out if we let it.

Make a contract like this:

"Show me an area of myself where I have a problem that really needs resolving so I can move forward with life."

Now look at the symbols.

If necessary, pick up each one in turn and ask yourself again, "Do I have a problem with (...)?"

Mostly, something will jump out at you right away.

Once you have the problem area, make a new set up - "Give me something today which will heal this, once and for all," and go forward into the resolving story from there.

Wishes, Wants, Needs & Desires

This is a great game to play at any time you're bored, dissatisfied, or you want to give yourself a real treat.

Here we use the symbols to communicate our wishes, wants, needs and desires.

We do so honestly, and without reservation; and we remember that what we are wanting, wishing for, wanting, needing and desiring does NOT have to be reasonable, it does NOT have to be practical, and you do NOT have to have any idea whatsoever of how such a thing could ever be achieved.

All you have to do is wish, want, need or desire **freely** – for once.

You can pick out random symbols, or do it in order; for each symbol let something come to you, for example:

"Time – oh I wish I had more time for my personal relaxation and creativity!"

"Space – I wish I lived in a bigger house, with spacious rooms and higher ceilings!"

"The Land – I really, really wish I could see the sky from my windows..."

... and so on.

It is quite a wonderful experience to get all that off your chest and out in the open.

But sometimes, you find requests that you can work with further, or that are an invitation to do more with that, explore it, let it lead you where it will.

Count Your Blessings

Use the symbols to focus on how you have been particularly blessed with time, friends, gifts, artefacts etc.

You can start with all the symbols face down, and lift one at a time, giving thought on what the blessings are and were, let examples, memories and ideas come streaming to you as to how you were blessed in this respect throughout your life.

Work your way through all 23 symbols and on each one, give grace for all the blessings you have specifically received.

If you can do energy work, you can let the power build a symbol at a time and finish with an overall gratitude to the enormity of all your blessings as you shift up and take the entire symbol sphere into consideration, all together.

A remarkable experience, indeed.

A lower level version of this is to make a contract that asks to be shown,

"What is really great about (our company, my husband, this school, this team, this product etc.)?"

When a group of people play this game, each symbol will produce many different responses from the different energy minds present; but as in the Blessings exercise, the power of the positive builds and builds into a truly amazing motivational experience that can change people's minds and hearts and attitudes profoundly in only a few short minutes.

The One Who Stands For Them All

This is a particular Project Sanctuary pattern that has no equal anywhere else.

Sometimes we have so many incidences of problems, memories or situations where the same thing happened over and over again, we end up feeling we have to be in therapy forever to resolve it all, one case at a time.

Big, global problems with many components are perfect for this pattern. For example, if a person had many relationships with many women and they were all abusive, we ask for ONE to come forward that "stands for them all" and if we resolved our relationship with THAT ONE today, then the rest would all fall, all be healed, in that instance, at the same time.

"Take me to the perfect place in time and space where I will meet the one that stands for them all."

Or if there were many incidences of abuse from one single person, we would ask for the one event that stands for them all.

If a person had innumerable problems with all sorts of different people, again we would ask for the one who stands for them all.

If a person has many, many aspects themed around one global problem (as is often the case with people who were abused once, and then it becomes a life pattern) we ask for the one aspect who stands for them all to be revealed so we can heal them and all is healed.

For a powerful business meditation, one might consider "the one customer who stands for the all" and meet with them, find out about their views, what they like and what they don't like, and listen to their suggestions for improvement.

This is a powerful pattern with many more applications than we might think; and a perfect example of something that we can't do consciously at all, but our energy minds can compute such complexity, and that is an awesome realisation..

Self Help & Personal Development

Please let me make it really clear one more time that ALL Project Sanctuary playing is about personal development.

We seek personal evolution through achieving threshold shifts as the outcome, goal and reason for playing with the Genius Symbols.

If you are being a therapist or magician or business coach and you are reading for another, this still benefits you directly as well as you learn more about these amazing processes and have the experience of the flow of new ideas, new stories and visions along the way, and it is very much you who benefits first from any threshold shifts that happen.

Even being in the presence of someone else's threshold shift is a powerful and uplifting experience; so whether you play for yourself, or help other people play their games with the symbols, you always get some form of personal evolution free of charge as well.

The same holds for all the healing games, whether you play them with yourself or with others; for all the creativity games of course, for everything in Sanctuary.

There are a few games of a very personal nature which are particularly powerful for personal development.

Adult Games

If your sex life isn't what it could be, there is probably something stuck somewhere; it might also be a case that your fantasy life isn't as rich and doesn't provide enough variety, interest and experiences as it might need to be to motivate you further.

Before you decide to skip this chapter as being irrelevant to you personally because you are (not interested in sex, in a loving relationship, fully sorted on the topic etc. et al) I would ask you to stop for a moment.

At an entirely structural level, the sexual energy channels in the energy body are extremely powerful. They are not just related to sex, but to all manner of other topics, from health to wealth, from happiness to success, and from status to self concept. This is so global and so wide spread that one might say, "Whatever the problem is you're having, do something with your sexual circuitry first. This changes the whole story 95% of the time. Should your problem be amongst the 5% minority that originates elsewhere, at least then you know that this is so and you can look elsewhere. But for 95% of the problems, it has been solved already in sexual circuitry, and if it had not been solved there, it would NEVER have been solved at all..."

For those who find the topic of sex scary, irrelevant or downright disgusting, just do a gentle set up like, **"Show me something sexy that is gentle yet profound and will really help me today."**

The Classic Game will give you a story that is, remember, custom made for you to learn something new, correct something, give you new ideas and forward momentum on stuck issues of all kinds.

Asking for a new fantasy lover to play with, asking for surprises in that context, finding new ways to play, **"Take me to the perfect place in time and space where I will experience the real joy of sex!"** and many more fabulous and interesting stories, ideas, journeys and feelings await you.

If you are particularly traumatised about sex, or if you are not, you can ask for a friend to come to you who will be the perfect personal guide to explore sex in a whole new way.

This is a particularly fascinating experience as your energy mind sends you someone who is calculated in real time and according to everything your energy mind knows about you.

First, make the contract of:

"Take me to the perfect place in time and space to meet my new friend who will help me evolve sexually."

Use the Classic Game to find the right habitat.

Once you have your habitat, you can use the "How To Make A Friend" instruction from the Genius Symbol chapter at the beginning of the book to co-create the right friend for you. Mostly however, you will find that a friend appears spontaneously in the habitat, even though you might have to look around a little to find them. A tip - not all frogs are just frogs in Sanctuary, if you know what I mean. ☺

Especially on a hot button topic such as sex, here is a great opportunity to really practice the right way to behave in Sanctuary.

Stay relaxed, monitor your stress levels and take action to de-stress and calm down. Remember that these are your worlds, all of this belongs to you and is under your power and command. Stay light, think in terms of this being a game and that you are playing, remember you have magic and you can change and shape anything here, and especially, remind yourself that **"This is all energy - and it's only energy."**

With that said, simply start to play!

I would add that adult games are amongst the most motivational forms of visions to help you unlock your autogenic abilities to really "come to life inside the data stream" and see, hear, feel, smell, touch, sense... everything in lucid clarity. Pretty amazing... ☺

Law & Order Games

Only we know what we've done, and what we've done wrong. There are many things spooking around within our data streams that we can't talk to anyone else about, don't want to talk or think about, but they need resolution.

Sometimes they need forgiveness, atonement – some THING that will move these events and incidences along so we can be free and clear, clean, as we step into the future.

> ***"Give me something that will help resolve the guilt over X."***

This will give all of you an opportunity to really come to terms with things and events, decisions, and bring you if not complete absolution, at least some kind of forward momentum again.

It is hugely relieving to even just be able to put those topics on the table and ask for help with whatever it is from your friends, the higher powers, from yourself.

Then there is the other side of the Law & Order games, namely that you have the opportunity in Sanctuary to bring people to justice at that level that you cannot touch in the hard.

Whether you want to do this in a vigilante fashion, or actually run a full trial in Sanctuary to get a resolution is up to you.

The systems of the human body and the human mind are extremely logical, extremely just - there is true law and order in the Universe, and no-one can break the universal laws that underlie everything. By playing law and order games in Sanctuary, we can regain that important sense of justice when this has become lost in our dealings with other humans; and to regain that sense of justice is a powerful evolution on many different levels.

Question Games

I once observed a person who had "low self esteem" and were constantly saying, thinking and acting on such statements as "I'm stupid," - "I'm no good," - "I'm ugly," - "I'm not smart enough," - "I'm lazy," - "I'm a waste of space," and so on, and on, and on, and on.

After a while I thought, that's pretty endless, where is all of that coming from?

All of it was coming from **one single underlying question**, which was, "Why did my mother give me away as a baby?"

All the statements of misery were simply answers to one single question at the bottom of it all. Take out the question, and the answers disappear; or you could replace the question to get different answers to be generated constantly and in the same fashion - **"Why am I so beloved by so many?"** for example. Play this contract and ask that question of every one of the 23 symbols and find out for yourself what that does to your self esteem and the way you view yourself.

"Give me a new question, perhaps the right question, the most important question, the most central question, the question that was never asked, but if it had been asked, would have answered so much..."

"Give me a question I should be asking today."

This contract, played with every one of the 23 symbols separately, will teach you a lot about questions.

Making contracts is also in a roundabout way a questioning skill; this is preceded by asking ourselves these questions that only the energy mind knows the answers to: "What is the time of day? What is the time of year? What is weather? What else is here..?"

Question games are **really** interesting on every topic and they are often the entrance point to a whole new realm of resources, ideas, inspirations and leading to new events in the hard, as well.

Playing For A Threshold Shift

In essence, we are always playing for threshold shifts – that's why we play Project Sanctuary.

When you make the set up that you are looking for a threshold shift in a particular area of your life however, we are being very direct and amazing things can and will happen as a result.

There is something quite magical about making the decision that "something has to be done about X!" in the first place; it denotes that you have become aware that there is a problem, and now we are activating the immense resources of Sanctuary to solve it.

You can be very specific when you are seeking a threshold shift, for example separating out one set of behaviours, a single occurrence or one thing that confuses you or that you don't understand.

What you will find, however, is that threshold shifts are immensely information dense and you get much, MUCH more than you originally expected or had bargained for, because whatever changes you are making in conjunction with your energy mind and your highest aspects are going to show you that what you were worried about was probably just the tip of the iceberg.

"Take me to the perfect place in time and space where I will experience a powerful threshold shift on the topic of..."

Playing For An Aspect

I discovered this interesting version of doing Genius Symbol readings one day when I had a little time on my hands, the symbols nearby but I couldn't think of what I wanted to do with them.

That's the "What are we having for dinner tonight?" moment when everything goes blank and all you want to do is not think about dinner at all!

I recognised it for what it was and as I was sitting at the kitchen table at the time, it was easy to imagine that there was another me sitting on the other side, in the traditional place of a querent if I was the traditional fortune teller.

I looked at the other Silvia and said, "Ah! What would you like help with today?" and she said, "I would like something to help me unblock my magic."

Yay! A question from the querent! A contract!

We can go to work... and we did, and it was a truly amazing experience that involved a long forgotten aspect who had a traumatic time with visions at a young age, and whom we could heal and help in a remarkable way.

Since I discovered this way of playing opposite the traditional empty chair, I have had wonderful experiences and results.

In the position of the querent, on the other side of the table from you, you can have aspects of yourself, your whole current self, a relative, dead or alive; even a friend or a hero of yours could be in the querent's chair, asking you a question and providing the contract, or the impetus for the idea for a contract.

This is also usable for Soul Pilot work and inviting ANY querent who might need your help on this day, if you are feeling brave.

Remember that every time you play the game in space and time, **you get better at it.**

You always gain something, you always learn something.

I really do recommend to play at least one game every day – do that for a week or a month and you will be AMAZED at the results that brings you.

Relationship Games

Relationships are complicated and very telling about ourselves; which is why many people will not tell the truth about their relationships to others, not even in the deepest therapy or their most trusted personal priest.

When we work with the symbols, we can be immensely truthful and also, we can be true to aspects that are normally not shown to anyone else.

"Give me something today to help me improve my relationship with X."

If you note, this phrasing of a contract may relate not just to a person, but is just as valid if you want to apply it to a substance abuse problem, an obsession, a fetish with an object, even an allergy.

Being able to honestly state what the problem is in a relationship without anyone sitting there and judging you for being truthful for once is a real godsend, and offers unprecedented opportunities for self healing in a totally private and protected setting.

"What can I do to improve my relationship with X?"

An important aspect of the 23 Genius Symbols is that they can show you 23 different points of views on one single problem, or one single situation. Or you could think of it as 23 different lenses that look at the same thing in different lights, and when you put them all together, a hugely much bigger picture emerges that is more than the sum of the parts.

That is the true power of the 23 symbols all together; and if you really want to change your mind about someone, or something, taking this amount of additional information into consideration will do that, and that's guaranteed.

"Take me to the perfect place in time and space where I and X can evolve our relationship to the next level."

This is an autogenic function of the Classic Game; you will meet with X in Sanctuary and the habitat you find yourself in will allow the two of you to learn more about each other and bring your relationship through to a threshold shift.

This is really awesome to experience, and it isn't "hard" - especially if you remain calm and remember that all is energy, and you have the power to change and morph everything you encounter.

You don't just have the power to do so, but that's your job as your conscious self, to go in there and to make the changes that need to be made. The energy mind cannot make these decisions for you; but it will work with you to show you if the decisions you make are beneficial or not. This becomes demonstrated in the feelings you have, and whether or not you are moving towards a threshold shift, or getting further away from it. You feel that in your body, in your emotions, you know when you're getting warmer, as the children's game goes; or colder, instead.

Do make a mental note of any topics or suggestions for games that you think might be "too hard" or "too advanced" or your response is, "Oh, I could never do THAT!"

That's just magic failure talking. These things are all easy, all light, and at the end of the day, they are all only energy.

"Take me to the perfect place in time and space to meet with X's higher self (or creative template)."

Relationship counselling in Sanctuary does not need to be confined to replicating some kind of therapy. Addressing the higher aspects of another person or entity is educational and leads to powerful threshold shifts that then ripple out into the hard and change things there as well.

As I sometimes say to people who have annoyed me, "I have been in touch with your higher self, and you'll be hearing from it shortly."

Tell Your Story

This is a totally fascinating game whereby instead of gaining a new story, you get to tell your energy mind about an old story using the symbols.

For example, if you were attacked when you were 12 years old in New York in Central Park, you would literally take the time symbol, place it down and say, "It was just after 10pm at night, the cinema had just finished."

Take the symbol for weather and say, "It was a cold November night, very clear, stars were out."

Take the symbol for the land and say, "I was walking down a street with tall buildings and before me lay the entrance to the park."

Take the symbol for the plants and say, "The trees were bare but the night wind was rustling in the bushes..."

Work your way through all the symbols until the entire story is told.

It is a truly extraordinary experience that completely changes things in a way that I can't put into words for you here, you'll have to do it to understand what that does.

In and of itself, that is one hell of a game; but now you have the story laid out in front of you, it has become a true Project Sanctuary story and you can change it.

You can ask, "What shall I do to change this first?" and let yourself be guided to a symbol that stands out to you.

When the story is changed, things are different in a whole new way.

Amazing.

Building A Visionary Goal

As in "Tell Your Story," here we use the symbols to build or refine a goal or vision.

This is very handy as we are telling the energy mind what we want in a way that it actually understands, something that was very difficult to do previously.

Goals can have different contexts of course and you will put that in the contract for the session; for example by saying out aloud, "This session is about my goals for prosperity and wealth."

Sit back and think for a moment of a scene or vision of you having achieved wealth in the widest possible sense but definitely including having stacks of real money as well.

Let's say we have the very common representation of drinking champagne on a yacht and getting a massage from handsome personnel while we're there.

Start with the basics and describe this scene to your energy mind, using the symbols from the Classic Game plus any others that help to set the scene and make it into a real habitat.

The time of day is just before lunch. The weather is fine. The land is the sea before a beautiful tropical island full of rain forest vegetation. The dwelling is in this case, the yacht. The other people are the captain and the scantily clad masseur. The artefact is a sparkling pure crystal goblet of the most expensive champagne on Earth that smells of grapes and tickles on your tongue... and so forth.

The Genius Symbols give you the opportunity to make this goal vision not just very real, but also to add detail and especially, the higher influences which are often lacking from "normal" goal setting procedures, such as having the helpful spirits of your ancestors there, supporting you, acting in accord with the higher powers of the universe and so forth.

If you develop the flat "ready to wear" goal "picture" of the yacht and all that into a proper habitat in which you can move around and have autogenic experiences, you can do many things with this.

For one, you can literally move in to your goal and live it for a while.

Do you really like spending all day on a yacht? Will you get bored? Will you miss your friends and family from back home, or the local cinema perhaps?

These and many other questions can and will be answered.

But there's more.

In Sanctuary, you are not alone.

Your energy mind is there too, and it can and will put a spanner in the works of that yacht dream if it doesn't agree with it, doesn't like it for whatever reason.

You might find, for example, that a tsunami is coming and it smashes the boat up, and you find yourself stranded on a lonely island that is nothing but sharp, barren rock with no vegetation and a lot of ugly, inedible birds screeching above.

Now, you may be disappointed - but the fact is that if your energy mind isn't on board (no pun intended!) with the yacht goal, you will never, ever get that anyway!

People spend a lifetime chasing the wrong goals and wonder why it never works, why it feels like endlessly pushing a boulder up the hill with no help from anyone, why they seem to "self sabotage" or why they're just never lucky when the moment comes...

Without our energy mind, no goal will manifest, it is as simple as that. Even if it did, as is often the case for surprise lottery winners, if the energy mind is not on board, you can see that new rich millionaire reality becoming eroded, quite literally, and as though it was nothing but an unstable Sanctuary construct, made from energy, that is falling apart.

It is fascinating to observe how that works.

If you should find out that your goal dream fantasy habitat is being broken, sabotaged or destroyed by the energy mind, you need to go back to the drawing board and find a new dream, a new goal.

"Give me the perfect place in time and space that will be my perfect goal to set me alight and draw me forward to be the best that I can be."

Now, we must remember that the conscious mind and the energy mind are equal partners in the greatest game on Earth.

If your energy mind takes you to a monastery and has you sitting in a grim unfurnished cell with a piece of stale bread and two cockroaches for company as that new goal vision, you have every right to reject that, to take yourself out of there and blow up the entire monastery.

That will tell the energy mind you didn't like that, just the same as the energy mind told you with the tsunami that it didn't like the yacht goal.

So you need to keep at it. These examples I'm giving you here are necessarily very black and white, very obviously wrong both ways; what you find more often is that with a little bit of give and take, and a few adjustments here and there, you and your energy mind get to agree on a goal.

Perhaps you can put a harbour on the tropical island with an airport next to it so you can visit the yacht and the island, but also jet around to other places which might include visiting your aged father on his birthday in the care home. Such a change might then cause in return the energy mind to reduce the tsunami to a storm that blows the yacht off course and doesn't completely destroy it on this occasion, just beaches it on a deserted island.

This is slightly better but still no agreement has been reached. You might then think that perhaps if your aged father was also on the island, in a super luxury nursing home and you can see him once a week instead of once a year, that there is no storm at all and the goal holds steady, the sun shines brightly and there may even be a beautiful rainbow to be seen over the sparkling turquoise ocean...

And we have learned something, a reason why the yacht goal alone wasn't motivational enough, and what was wrong with it; as well as what was needed to fix it so it would be acceptable to all of you as a goal.

It's fascinating to dance with the energy mind in this way.

When we do, we get given solutions and answers that are so profound, so wise, so astonishing and so beautiful, it really takes the breath away and leaves us wondering how else we would have ever been able to learn that, to find out the truth about that.

Finding good goals to work towards is a very motivational thing to do; it is also very powerful at the multi-level.

If you can find a goal for yourself that pleases all of you, where is no resistance remaining, and both your conscious mind and your energy mind have come into harmony, first of all you will experience a powerful threshold shift. You will understand so much more about yourself in moment of enlightenment and you will get the body sensations to match. What happens next is that a lot of chaos, conflict and the aforementioned self sabotage just disappear from your life.

Things are become easier, smoother. Luck and synchronicity starts to play a part in your endeavours, and it seems as though there were invisible hands helping and guiding you along the way.

That would be the effect of both you and your energy mind being on the same page, working towards the same goal/s.

Should you become discouraged, tune into your new shared goal; it will be powerfully motivating, resonant, and will take on a life of its own. This new goal also has another amazing feature, namely that it will evolve with you, morph and change as you yourself evolve. In that way, the new goal will remain relevant and become a reality in your life from the moment the threshold shift has occurred and long before it has physically become manifest.

Well, well worth doing, and doing sooner, rather than later.

Creativity

Well, where do we start?

Project Sanctuary is intelligent, infinite creativity in essence – but you can add another dimension by using contracts.

This puts you totally in charge of your creativity; it makes the highest, most visionary forms of creativity reliable and accessible to ANY HUMAN BEING who functions well enough to be able to read these words.

That is quite unprecedented in the history of humanity; enjoy this fact as you play with the Genius Symbols to unlock your very own true and amazing flows of creativity with ease.

Stories

"Give me the story that helps me overcome problems x."

"Give me a story for X that will help him/her with their problem X."

"Give me the perfect story for a five year old boy who has been sexually abused to help him heal."

"Give me a new story that is a Wild West story for a film script."

"Give me the right story to tell this audience that will make them understand."

"Give me a cool story I can develop into a best selling computer game."

"Give me a story that helps me write this sales page."

"Give me a story for this new TV advertisement."

"Give me a story that holds the key to understanding X."

"Give me a story to deepen my connection with X."

"Give me a story that teaches me something important today."

"Give me a story to tell my 12 year old aspect so they get over X."

"Give me the perfect story to tell to this one person here, right now."

"Give me a story that excites me and energizes me."

"Give me a story that will help me to go to sleep."

"Give me 23 stories for my brand new book of fairy tales, one per symbol."

"Give me a story that will change my life."

As the contracts are endless, so are the stories...

If you are new or unused to the concept of "the story," or if you are amongst those people who were told that only facts count and stories are nothing, or lies, if you will, let me encourage you to start "thinking story."

Literally everything has a story.

There are short stories such as the life of a fly that lives only for one day; and long stories such as that of the Earth from the beginning, with many chapters, each one of which are stories as well.

Everything has a story, and every existence in the Universe tells a story.

Even "facts" tell stories.

A story is a sequence of moments in time, one after the other; and all the stories of everything there is are intertwined with each other.

Stories flow and they are immensely information rich; you could say that only the story really tells you all you need to know about something. An equation in isolation means very little; if you add more equations, there is more information. But it is not until you add the story of where these equations came from, who made them, and what they are being used for that the "bigger picture" begins to emerge and the true story is beginning to be told.

The energy mind works in and with stories - our flow of data, our energy streams rich and dense with information.

People are designed to learn by and communicate through stories, even if these stories have been abbreviated into a short word, such as "cat" - behind that word there lie a million stories and more, of living beings that move, evolve, interact with their environments, have come from somewhere and are going somewhere still.

Without the energy mind to help us out, these stories are too much, too complex, too information dense, too intertwined and this is why we have consciously started to reduce reality, to cut it up into pieces in the hope that the information overwhelm will be containable.

With the energy mind on board, stories make sense; indeed, they are the only way to understand anything properly at all.

So when I tell you story, or I ask you to tell a story, I would like you to remember that you are not regressing to a state of simplistic, unrealistic children's thinking, but progressing into the most complex, beautiful and information dense thinking environment known to mankind.

If you can feel comfortable in the world of stories, you can feel comfortable in any thinking endeavour which pales into insignificance in comparison.

Stories too are logical, and once you discover that for yourself, and you begin to discover stories everywhere, the world will never seem the same again, and the true potential of our natural, existing genius does become revealed.

So by all means, create stories. Live stories. Use stories as the complex, elegant and astonishing tools they are to help us evolve in any field, any time, in any situation - anywhere.

On a personal note I would add that I live in the hope that more people will make their way to their own energy mind, and bring back stories, new stories, that will become the films and books, songs and plays, articles, facts and sciences that will excite us, delight us, and enrich us all.

"Better Stories"

"Now my story is fair done,

I beg you: tell a better one!"

This phrasing was used amongst story tellers of old as they were taking their turn in telling their stories, passing the spotlight from one to the other.

It was a challenge of course, and it was then as it is in this game designed to bring out new resources and stretch our ability to simply make "better" stories – however you want to define that.

Richer stories, longer, more concise; more meaningful, more exciting; more information dense, more transformative, containing more and more powerful threshold shifts; more applicable for the audience, more sellable, more profitable – how do you want to define your "better stories"?

You can leave it with the thought to ask just for a better story in general, like the old story tellers did, and you might find improvements that you didn't expect and couldn't even foresee or think to ask of.

Time Games & Time Stories

I don't know yet why or how it is that when you set the time, the rest of the story follows so easily; and it doesn't matter of course as we are interested in the stories, the threshold shifts and their practical results at this point, rather than the potential theory.

In fairy tales, time and space are set with "Once upon a time, in a kingdom far away."

If you place your story there using the symbols and defining time and space to be THAT, you end up with the fairy tale plane, a land outside of time and space altogether, where very metaphorical things are happening.

In Project Sanctuary, as soon as you have the time – time of day and time of year if we are playing on Planet Earth or something like it! - you have the location and the entire habitat is there.

So it is possible to steer the story from the time angle.

You can place the time symbol and state a time of your choice, like you would set the dial on a time machine, to go to a time of your choosing.

This can be a Science Fiction type future, it can be any actual date in Earth's history, it can be more global to an era like the Middle Ages or the Roman times, and it can be a precise time and date from your own memories, or that of anyone you are dealing with.

This is useful and really interesting for unfolding and creating everything from a Wild West TV series to a Science Fiction novel, a memory retrieval for a court case, a psychic reading or a finding, or a meditation involving the real Egyptian magical ceremonies you want to learn more about.

The ability to steer the story with great specificity from the time angle gives you a lot of control and flexibility over your visions and makes it much easier to get outstanding results with your stories and inquiries.

23 New Games

On the topic of a time game, we do have 23 symbols, not just time.

A game is something that you play; you might play it alone, or with other people. A game might be a computer game or a board game, and it may be adult in nature, or very simple like Snakes & Ladders; or simple and complex at the same time, as would be the case with chess; or something that is more like a sport, such as billiards or very much like a sport, such as football.

As an exercise in creativity, have a thought and an enquiry for one new game per symbol and find out what you energy mind has to say on the topic.

You can choose your details level very precisely, such as stating you only want computer games for 18+ single players; or you can leave it wide open and ask for a new game, and let yourself be surprised.

This is an excellent game to play with children and with your own inner child too; and an excellent practice piece to get a good answer on each symbol.

> *Tip:*
>
> *If nothing comes to you when you consider the symbol and ask the question/state the contract, play a full Classic Game because there is a blockage that requires a threshold shift to give you the answer, solution or idea.*

Creative Writing, Poetry & Paranormal Language

Having worked with visions for a long time now, and in my capacity as an author, having written down the main gist of a vision on many occasions, I have come to the conclusion that the holy grail of written and spoken communication is what I now call "paranormal language".

Paranormal language can't be constructed by the rules of grammar; it occurs **naturally and spontaneously** when we describe visions in real time.

Please note that I said "in real time" - this means to describe the vision at the same time as it is happening (as opposed to having the vision in the garden, taking a nap, having dinner first, and then sitting down to remember what it was like to have had the vision some hours earlier).

When you are inside the data stream and consciously experiencing the events that happen, and you comment on these events there and then, grammar goes out of the window and we start to speak and think in a very different way. This different way of thinking and speaking (which turns into writing if you do it there and then) produces unusual language occurrences, unique language occurrences which are above and beyond the normal mundane level of speaking and writing.

These are occurrences of paranormal language, and they are the goal and prize of all creative writing.

Paranormal language has nothing to do with being very clever, or knowing a lot of long or complicated words. It has nothing to do with being crazy or stirring up words and grammar like a schizophrenic salad of frogs, ashes and washing powder in a blender.

- **Paranormal language happens when our conscious words start to align with the energy mind visions and when that happens, paranormal language is the only way to speak, think or write.**

In order to produce any kind of true creative writing, be this prose, dialogue, poetry or ad copy that sizzles, we need to write from within the data stream of the vision.

As you will remember, I have encouraged you right from the beginning to describe the answers and visions you are getting **out aloud in words.**

Just as we have to get used to streaming smooth, flowing visions, we have to get used to streaming smooth, flowing words to describe these visions. It is simply a practice matter and becomes very easy and natural with the smallest amount of practice.

It becomes easy and natural because it is easy and natural for people to speak in a flow of words, a sing-song of words to express their intrapersonal reality.

Recently, a researcher in a British school undertook a project to improve the reading and writing skills of ten year old boys which were globally lagging behind girls in their abilities and their test scores.

After four weeks, the researcher had a breakthrough, or a threshold shift, as we call it – he realised that they boys didn't know how to talk, and if you don't know how to talk, of course, you can't write, and your can read fluently either.

The basis of all creative writing is the ability to talk in the first place, the ability to describe the world in words that flow, one after the other, and are indeed a part of the data stream of experience, not even an addition.

If you find talking out aloud about what you see, hear, feel, taste, sense and scent in the visions and memories your energy mind sends you is a particular challenge, I would strongly encourage you to use a modern energy psychology technique such as EFT Emotional Freedom Techniques or EmoTrance to help you de-stress and remove some of these blockages.

You can also use the symbols themselves in healing, therapy and memory games to remove that blockage and allow the flow of the spoken word to start up,

Once you can start to speak about your visions and describe them as they are happening, don't censor or judge yourself in any way as the main purpose is at this point to create the flow. That is exactly the same for speaking the words as it is for the flow of visions and impressions themselves.

You can record what you said and transcribe it later on, and what you will find is that amongst the things you said, pretty much right from the start, there are descriptions and sequences of words that are so poetic, so artistic, so resonant, so right and so powerful that you are quite astonished when you hear them back.

That is the spontaneous occurrence of paranormal language at work.

You know such phrases are amazing because you can feel them in your body; and other people can feel them too.

Here is an example of an occurrence of paranormal language in one of my fairy tales which I remember well delighted me much at the time, and which is still a really nice sequence and an example of a piece of writing that is nothing more than the best description I could give of the vision I had at the time:

> *And so time passed, and then more time; it slipped down the stream from the mountain side; it melted like the clear, tipped icicles in spring; it rushed like autumn leaves and crackled like cosy fires in the hearth when storms came sweeping down across the meadow.*[6]

As you become more accustomed to streaming visions and describing them, and as your conscious mind and your energy mind get more and more on the same page, you will find more occurrences of paranormal language and they come closer together too.

This is a natural process and you don't have to do anything other than to **honestly** tell about your experiences from within the data stream.

---

[6] Excerpt from "The Star Child" fairy tale from "The Golden Horse & Other Stories" DragonRising 2006.

- **Honesty is the key in true creative writing based on the vision stream.**

Don't try and be clever; simply be honest and describe what you feel, hear, see, sense, scent, touch and taste as best you can.

Coupled with the unique quality of the visions themselves, you can't help but create creative writing, extremely poetic writing, sharp and logical prose as a side effect with just a little bit of practice.

For experienced authors and poets, you can ramp up your expectations of what you can achieve by paying attention to the contracts you make with your energy mind; you can create contracts that are designed to expand your abilities to not just produce "stream of consciousness" poetry and writing, but to shape and form that in the translation process into words in any way you choose.

You can stipulate for example to be given a vision for a poem and it must be a perfectly formed sonnet when it's done.

"Give me a new sonnet that will amaze me."

Obviously, you can choose any style or form of writing that you wish; I've done iambic pentameter exercises in this way, obviously haikus, the aforementioned sonnets and all manner of really obscure poetic meters when I first found out that you can do that – make a contract and both conscious and energy mind co-operate and give you exactly what you asked for.

This form of creative writing is by no means confined to the poetic. With the pure information processing and delivery power of the energy mind in sync with the conscious mind, you can do things like, "Take this list of the top 50 keywords relating to metaphor and produce an article that is entertaining and educational for children who know nothing, but would keep an NLP Master Trainer amused, and while we're there, teach me something I didn't know yet."[7]

---

[7] This article actually exists and you can find it at http://silviahartmann.com/metaphor-article-metaphor-course.php

Creative writing is extremely important and powerful; and whether you want to employ it to write your definitive trilogy (as I did with In Serein, a full 500,000 words novel which had a unique contract up front) or whether you want to write the definitive love letter; whether you want to write an advertisement that really gets people's attention or you want to write a speech that will gain a standing ovation – yes, you can have it all, it isn't even that difficult.

Practice your visions, practice speaking out aloud what you experience, get that flow going, make your contract with your mind and allow yourself to be blown away by what you can do with "creative writing" and of course, "creative public speaking" in the end.

I am still in awe of how these simple, basic skills keep on evolving over time, and neither of us would be here today if I hadn't taken the time to practice and hone my skills of visioning, and creative writing!

Design, Illustrations & Paintings

Don't skip this section because you don't think of yourself as artistic in that arty way that pertains to design, illustration, paintings and sculptures.

To me, being a genius doesn't mean being a one trick pony who is good at one tiny limited thing; being a real genius is bringing a touch of true genius to everything you touch.

When we start to step out of our comfort zones, whatever they may be, and try some of the other modalities of expression that are on offer to all human beings, we don't just learn all sorts of new skills and gain more mental flexibility.

You will find when you come back to your original modality, you have noticeably improved in that as well.

So if you want to be a better mathematician, poet or engineer, allowing yourself to play with other modalities will be the way forward – as well as a whole lot of fun.

Creating brand new, innovative, creative, stunning designs, illustrations, paintings and sculptures is easy – they are just translations of our friends, the multi-modality visions, into those shapes and forms.

Here is how to do it.

Once you have your story, you can pick out the most memorable/ powerful/resonant single images and turn them into paintings, sculptures and all manner of works of art.

You can abstract them to any degree, just have a few lines here, a few colours there, or go to town and really paint the scene like Michelangelo; either way, these will all be amazing and totally original works of art that have the depth of a true visionary story behind them.

The act of finding particularly resonant images in a stream of visions in and of itself is quite an interesting ability which you can practise, even or even especially if you have no interest in art or painting at all, by the following method.

When the story is done and you've had your threshold shift, ask yourself which one image, if you took a still photographic image or froze time there, matrix style, would really sum up the spirit of the whole story for you? Where is that special moment when the emotions were highest, or which was particularly meaningful for you?

Get the scene clear in your mind. Ask questions about it, pay attention and refine it until the scene is so real and steady that you could walk right into it if you wanted to.

Now take a simple piece of paper and place some simple geometric shapes that represent the main components of the scene; such as two lines for a river, a triangle for a mountain, a few zig zags for a bridge, the sun in the sky and two ovals for the two people who stood on the bridge, as simple as that.

It is a very interesting experience to jot down in a few strokes and simple geometric figures a kind of pictorial "note to self" of that key moment in the story. It enhances many key skills that will stand a visionary genius in good stead over time, and even with the simplest of shapes on the paper, you have created a work of art that is based on visionary genius.

- **Your drawing is unique, it came from within, it is not a copy of someone else's ideas or visions; it is yours and there is a whole story behind it.**

That is my definition of art[8]. It is entirely truthful, free from pretence and powerful from the moment a person first attempts it. Whether or not a person has technical skills in the modality, be it drawing or painting, illustrating, designing or sculpting, making clothes based on visions or whatever else is the final outcome that always and only starts with an original vision, is a totally different story.

---

[8] For more information about energy art, art solutions and visionary art in practice please see www.1-art.eu

The important thing to remember in the context of art especially is that when you have your visions under control, as we do when we make a contract with the energy mind, gain a vision, and then refine the vision by stepping into the data stream and engaging with it from within until a threshold breach occurs, is that the contract controls what kind of work of art you will be producing in the end.

You can choose whether you want to make works of art that appal and disgust, or inspire and intrigue; you are no longer at the mercy of trying to force visions through drugs, pain or madness. Likewise, your works of art will be logical and resonant, and fit for the purpose you made them for, whatever that may be.

I'd like to mention that the geometric placement of the most important elements of the vision is of course what gives you symbols and abstract designs which can be used to create everything from jewellery, to logos for businesses, and from esoteric symbols for your own purposes to elegant designs that are simple yet extremely information rich.

With this basic pattern of first having a vision, flash or story, picking out one particular scene that is the most resonant, or has the most meaning for you, and then rendering that scene and its major components in a simple, geometric fashion, you have the entrance route into the world of visual arts.

There is much of interest there, and it is simple enough to add this particular genius string to your evolving genius bow.

Sculpture

If painting and illustrating is the "seeing" modality rendering of a full modality vision, then the sculpture is the "touching" modality plus seeing in 3D. If your sculpture produces some kind of sound, you have that modality as well to represent a vision.

For many people, the idea of creating a sculpture is even more alien than to draw a few geometric shapes; and why this should be valuable even more of a mystery.

I like to take the "Why do you climb a mountain?" - "Because it's there and I can!" approach to all forms of expressing an original vision in one of the physical shapes, forms and crafts human beings have invented over the millennia.

It makes sense to consider that if you have never sat down with a lump of clay and asked your hands to shape it into something that is representative of a visionary experience, you will be activating pathways in your brain, in your mind and in your body that you might have never used before.

I hold that the more such pathways we have, the more intelligent we become; the more freely information streams and flows around our systems; the more connections are being made, the more multi-dimensional our internal map of the universe becomes, and the more we become able to manifest, influence and control objects and events in the hard.

Making an object from clay that you shape with your hands and making it based on a vision is an amazing experience, and not as difficult as you might think – all we have to do to get us going with this alien modality is to ask the symbols for a vision or a story that will tell us what to make, and encourage us to make it because it is exciting, inviting, fascinating, and we can't not have a go.

You don't have to work in clay, either. Sculpture is anything three dimensional; you can make a totem by combining objects to create a sculpture, or use any material you are drawn to, or that might be suggested in the content of a vision, flash or memory.

A wonderful, meditative endeavour to play by yourself, in a group, with children; to become more intelligent, to learn something new, to have fun, but in the end, **simply because you can.** ☺

Music

Most people find it quite easy to match a little picture or a painting to a PS story or vision, but haven't thought that it is just as easy to match a little song, a composition or an entire symphony.

You can take any musical instrument such as a recorder, piano, mouth organ or whatever you have to hand and simply try a few notes, to find one that resonates with the story or vision.

As with the pictures and sculptures, it is a visceral "yes/no" process that is amazingly positive and accurate.

"Does this note match?"

You can feel yes and no immediately. Keep trying one note after the other until you get a "Yes!"

Now, you've got one note, so what happens next? Another will follow, and then another, until you have a melody and that makes a song.

The first time you do this it is totally amazing how you could possibly know, especially if you haven't ever had anything to do with music; but it's just energy, and matching up energy is something we can all do, and easily so.

If you don't have a musical instrument, try humming a few notes and phrases. Keep the story/vision in mind and simply feel for a match. It's a fascinating process and creates amazing and once again, completely original songs.

Ideas

How many ideas do you want? You can have endless ideas, from an entire story, or very specifically for one purpose or to solve a problem, or to answer a question.

Turning the symbols face down and asking for an idea for X, drawing a symbol and letting it take you from there will generate as many ideas as you could ever want or need.

As before, the contract steers the process in the right direction -

"Give me an idea for X." or

"Give me an idea for X that the client will love!" or

"Give me a new idea for X which will be incredibly successful!"

Be brave, have faith – and let your own energy mind ASTONISH you, time and time again as you get one idea per symbol and you end up with 23 ideas on every contract, easily so. If you need even more ideas, ask for three ideas per symbol – real energy mind creativity is really infinite.

An important reminder:

Do NOT dismiss ideas or as we call it, "send them back" as being pointless, or substandard, or too (whatever). You need to take the idea or vision or story and say, "Thank you," then move on immediately. If you do that, you'll get more, you'll get better at it, and you get to be more precise with your contracts as well over time.

If you have to send an idea or a vision back, don't do it in a rejectful manner. Ask for further refinements instead, for new developments, or changes even in the deepest structure, if necessary.

Keep the lines of communication OPEN and FLOWING, back and forth – that's how you get eventual agreement between the conscious mind and the energy mind, and a truly fabulous idea, invention, resolution as a result of the PROCESS of communication.

Dealing With An Overflow Of Ideas

Something interesting that we found after we've had the Genius Symbols for a while was that people didn't know how to cope with that many ideas, or how to deal with them, or how to choose amongst them.

With hindsight, this stands to reason.

Good, original, visionary ideas are so far and few between in human cultures as it stands at the moment, we are still recycling Science Fiction stories and superheroes that were created a hundred years ago and no-one seems to be able to come up with something better – and there are supposedly 8 billion people on Earth at the moment.

So it stands to reason that people never developed skills and strategies to deal with infinite information on tap and become overwhelmed when instead of just one good idea, once in a lifetime, you milk for all it's worth until you stagger around in a Zimmer frame, you have 23 ideas in front of you, right here and now, and each one could be developed into something amazing, and you know that.

There is another aspect to this.

23 is quite a lot to handle in consciousness; indeed, there are some who say that one may only be able to hold 7 +-2 bits of information in the conscious mind at any one moment in time.

We are playing with the 23 Genius Symbols in order to bring the conscious mind and the energy mind together so they start to work together.

I have mentioned this before, but it really is central to understand that we are not working with visions in the old way, where a vision is downloaded into the conscious mind, and now the conscious mind tries to figure out what to do with that all by its lonesome self.

We can apply the “more than the sum of the parts” power of the energy mind and the conscious mind working in harmony also to the question as to what we are going to do with all that information, with all those ideas, and in which order and sequence.

The simplest way of all to choose one from a list of 23 ideas is to go back to the Genius Symbols and ask, "Which one do I find the most attractive? Which one do I like the best?"

A symbol will jump out at you, or you will be drawn towards it.

The idea that corresponded to that symbol on this occasion is the one you are most attracted to.

In this way, you can sort your information, using questions and contracts to get to know your information better and take it beyond 23 single, disconnected ideas.

You can ask the entire set each time:

"Which idea is the most commercially successful?"

"Which idea is the easiest and quickest to implement?"

"Which idea would be the most fun to work with?"

"Which idea would open the doors to more beneficial events in the long run?"

"Which idea would please X the most?"

"Which idea would be the most likely to develop into something new we haven't even thought of yet?"

"Which idea is the most powerful overall?"

"Which idea can help us now the most?"

"Which idea should we implement first?"

"Which idea should be keep for next year?"

"Which ideas should be worked on together and in sync?"

Make a note of the symbol answers without referring back to the idea itself to keep it clean, then consider what you've got.

Sometimes, the same symbol turns up repeatedly; for example, if your 23 ideas were for a new product, the same symbol might come up as the most fun to work with, and the most commercially successful, and the one that might please the boss the most.

Clearly, this is the stand out idea that wants to be paid the most attention to.

However, I want to encourage you to not ever just hunt for **"the one"** good idea, or the one good story, or the one breakthrough innovation, or the one of anything at all.

The endless quest for the one is all based on the poverty of ideas that used to exist without the energy mind in the frame.

It is perfectly possible to have more than one good idea, and to take note and apply more than one good idea either sequentially or simultaneously.

If your project is vision driven, you can work on more than one project at a time, at the same time, without ever losing focus, because you can switch between the visions that hold it all together at will.

You can have three or more books to be written as documents open on your desktop at the same time and switch between them with ease, as and when you feel like it. In the impoverished world of the "one good idea in a lifetime" this is inconceivable; but when your energy mind is on board, it's easy, natural, and I would even say, the right way to work.

Likewise, you can have many projects going on at the same time, and work on many different ideas, all of which have their timeline, their evolution, their causes and effects, and many of which will eventually come together, connect up, cross-fertilise each other and create that typical energy mind driven result of **becoming more than the sum of their parts.**

The moral of the story is: Don't be afraid of having too many good ideas than you can handle. You can handle more than five, fifty, five thousand good ideas, and easily so, if you bring your energy mind into the game. The energy mind can handle infinite complexity, calculate that for you and give you its calculations.

In order for it to be able to do that for you, and in order for you to learn how to think in that new way, and most importantly, to learn to rely on your energy mind giving you ideas and answers that are genius in every way you want to define that, you need to play the games.

You need to practice and get used to communicating with your energy mind.

So by all means, do the "23 good ideas for X" generation game often, and don't stop there, play on with your results. Learn to get comfortable with having a lot of data, and how to query that data in all kinds of different ways.

If your energy mind goes on strike, chances are you are over thinking everything and not listening enough, not asking enough questions before you jump to conclusions.

Should that happen, apologize sincerely to your energy mind, find a new contract and simply start all over again with a better attitude, with a lighter, friendlier, more relaxed attitude.

The light will come back, and with it, that proverbial light bulb that goes on in people's heads when they have found yet another genius solution.

The Ideas Habitat: The Tesla Machine

As Project Sanctuary habitats are energetic reconstructions of actual reality, they can be used to run virtual simulations called Tesla Machines, after the genius inventor Nikola Tesla who would create machines in Sanctuary first, run them there, then take them apart to see the wear and tear. By the time he handed in the blueprints for the actual physical machines to be built, they were perfect and worked perfectly in the hard.

Nikola Tesla built machines; but that is actually simple compared to running a Tesla machine that calculates the behaviour of an entire population, an entire market place, a whole business, a family or even just one particular human being.

I must make the note to beginners that one must not confuse a Sanctuary habitat running a Tesla Machine with conjecture or day dreaming; when the energy mind is calculating the variables and the evolution of any habitat, the results are extremely impressive.

In the context of testing ideas in a Sanctuary environment before we take the blueprints to be created in the hard, and spend much time and money on any given project or single idea, we simply have to make sure that the testing habitat is stable and well defined.

It is important to note that all and any aspects of a habitat are a part of the Tesla Machine we are building; not just the "machine itself". What I mean by that is to know that the entire habitat, in Nikola Tesla's example the workshop habitat he built, in the time and place he built it in, all the tools in that habitat, all the other helpers there, every nail in the roof and every board on the floor are as much a part of the Tesla Machine as are the actual machines in the middle of the workshop space.

- **The entire habitat functions as a Tesla Machine.**

Let us say you had an idea for a particular kind of hand bag to be sold in your accessories shop.

In order to test this idea using a Tesla Machine, you would build a habitat, using the Genius Symbols and the Classic Game, which includes the street where your shop is located, and the shop itself which features the new design of handbags in the window.

Now we let the habitat run and observe the reactions of the passing public to the new handbags. We may listen in to their comments, note what buying decisions they make; even watch the staff interact with interested parties and what happens when they try to sell these bags to customers, old and new alike.

We can move time in the habitat and let a number of months pass; we can then enter the office of the shop and look at the sales figures over time, or according to season, to get a long term view of what effect the introduction of the new line of handbags may have had.

If you have never done anything like this before, it may sound complex; impossible; but I must keep on reminding you that you're not doing this alone; that your energy mind is the real engine behind any Tesla Machine; and that with that engine on board and a little focus of your conscious mind you really can learn new things about the future and viability of any given idea without ever doing a single thing in the hard.

There is so much you can do with this, and all of it is simply fascinating.

Once your shop habitat in our example is established, you can do much more than just test a single idea without risk of any kind. You can use it to test out all manner of changes safely and before you implement anything in the hard. You can change the décor, you can change the staff, you can train the staff, and when something doesn't work out in the habitat, you can be pretty sure it wouldn't work in the hard, either.

Tesla Machines of this kind can go much further, of course. You can experiment here in a risk free way, and also invite in friends and advisers, and gain new ideas from inside the habitat itself. It is a truly fascinating thing to do, and I encourage you highly to build a replica of something that you are interested in, be it the kitchen table with the six kids fighting at dinner time, the marriage bedroom, the office you work in, the business or department you run, your laboratory, your garden, your work room, your kitchen.

Once you have built a good replica of a hard environment as a habitat, you are ready to experiment in and with that habitat.

Start by introducing some new elements and find out what happens in and to the habitat when you do that.

As a beginner, start with some more drastic changes to make the effects on the habitat clearly noticeable to you; here is a chance to play, and to have fun. Stay light. Enjoy being silly sometimes, injecting some humour into the habitat can break old entrained habits of mind beautifully and open the door to much more realistic and powerful insights.

Tesla Machine habitats are endlessly fascinating and very useful for every day life both for personal as well as professional development and success; and I can tell you that we would not have the Genius Symbols without them.

Problem Solving

A problem is a puzzle; and using the symbols to give a new perspective on any problem is a fascinating thing to do.

Focus on your problem and draw a symbol.

Let your energy mind go into action and show you something that is highly relevant to your problem in hand. Most of the time, the first symbol you draw already does the trick; but you can refine your solutions by drawing further symbols to create a story solution for your problem.

You can also create a custom habitat to help you solve your problem.

Define the time and landscape, the components and actors that exist in and around the problem, such as recreating your office with all the co-workers and the boss in Sanctuary, or the competition swimming pool, or a model or the whole system you are working on.

Once you have turned any situation or problem into a habitat, you can move around in it, change it and work with it in any way you like.

For example, you can run the same scene or sequence of events many times, and until you get your required outcome or something even better still, using the habitat as an advanced and interactive Tesla Machine.

If you are wondering what to wear for this year's fancy dress party, use the classic game symbols to create the habitat correctly, the office, all the workers, have them drink as they should and then open the door and watch you stepping inside dressed as a cowboy. Observe the reactions, and re-set the game back to the moment just before the door opens; this time, you're wearing a Big Bird costume instead.

Because this is Sanctuary and not a fear fuelled hallucination, it will give you an extremely accurate reading that reflects what will really happen in the hard perfectly and reliably.

Over time and practise, this process can get very fast, near enough automatic, and can generate endless scenarios until the perfect breakthrough solution has been found.

Inventions

"Give me a new invention today!"

A great game, one that children just love, and whether you play this for fun or for profit, it is a great open invitation for your energy mind to come forward and prove to you just what it is capable of – if only we think to ask it.

A true invention is something that never existed before and that's a cool thing to ask for in a vision.

But you can also do innovation instead, which is taking an existing thing and simply making it better.

There isn't one single thing that humans are currently using that couldn't be innovated to make it better in every sense of the word you want to use.

More user friendly. More environmentally friendly. More profitable. More beautiful. More logical. Easier to transport, easier to clean, easier to build, easier to dispose of.

On this one, the world is your oyster in the true sense of the metaphor.

And do know that we are all waiting with baited breath for the next innovation that will solve an existing problem, even one we weren't aware we were experiencing.

Innovate and invent away – you'll be doing us all a favour!

Divination

Traditional Psychic Readings & Oracles

The Genius Symbols make the mysterious processes of "reading the tea leaves," "gazing into the crystal ball" or "reading the Tarot Cards" as easy as pie.

Sit opposite the querent and ask them to focus on their problem or what they need to have help with.

Simply read off the "classic Project Sanctuary adventure game" symbols in order; let the story come to you and just tell it as you see/hear/feel it unfold.

The querent will come in at some point and make the story their own; you can then assist them to come to a threshold shift on their presenting problem.

Another version is to place the symbols face down and let the querent mix them up before you pick up one symbol at a time and read it as you go along. It's easy and amazing in the depth of information that comes forth, and even in the hands of a beginner, will give the querent a most amazing experience the like of which they've never had before.

Of course, you can also let the querent choose any number of symbols and use those to give you the vision that's required.

If you are a tarot reader, you can use the symbols in the patterns of tarot readings, such as the Celtic Cross, or the houses of the Zodiac.

You'll get quite unprecedented and stunning results because the Genius Symbols are so easy and so directly understood.

Predictions & Psychic Phenomena

Through the contracts, you can use your Genius Symbols and processes to give you information and readings on just about anything you want to. For example you could ask...

"Show me what lies in the future for X"

Or...

"Give me information about what is going on in this haunted house"

More than that, the interactivity of the data stream also gives you the ability to do something about whatever it is – you get to respond to the information you are receiving.

This is particularly useful for bad futures and haunted houses; just knowing what is going on is clearly not enough!

Improving Psychic Abilities

We all want to improve our psychic abilities and our abilities to be absolutely in charge of these, as well – no-one wants to be inundated with spirits all the time, after all.

This in and of itself is the major reason why we tend to block our psychic abilities, often at a very young age when it first becomes apparent that there's more to the world than meets the eyes of day.

"Give me something today which will help restore and improve my psychic abilities!"

...is a great contract that you can play with yourself and in groups many times to find places where your systems might need healing, re-arranging, or what kind of extra energies, events and experiences are needed to really catalyse your psychic circuitry to a whole new level.

Highly recommended!

Remote Viewing

"Take me to location X."

Remote viewing using the Genius Symbols is as easy as to state the location in time and space you wish to view, and then playing the Classic Game to make the remote location arise as a habitat.

There really isn't much more to be said about it; the Classic Game takes all the mental contortions out of remote viewing and makes it accessible and simple to anyone who wishes to use this.

Dreams & Dream Interpretation

Any dream is a habitat! If the dream is remembered, the correct procedure is to re-enter the dream and play the story on, forward, to a threshold shift.

You can use the symbols to guide yourself or another to the correct resources, and order and sequence of what we have to do to resolve the dream and "get the message" - which does NOT become apparent before the dream has been successfully resolved.

That's where general dream interpretation goes so very wrong, trying to guess the moral of the story from the first act alone. A remembered dream is an invitation from the energy mind to communicate and work together, and when we do that, dream resolutions can be truly fabulous tools towards growing into who we are supposed to be.

Dream resolutions PS style are wonderfully empowering and this is a game to play with children so they learn from a young age how to deal with scary dreams in such a way that they are totally and positively resolved, leaving you far smarter, calmer and more knowledgeable than if you'd never had that scary dream at all.

You can lay out the dream to start you off as in "Tell Your Story" in the Therapy section by placing the requisite symbols in order as you re-create the dream event as a Project Sanctuary habitat – and then you go on to evolve it towards a visionary resolution.

<u>Note:</u>

Dreams evolved in that way NEVER return! You might get new dreams that re-visit the habitat but the old dreams are gone, because they are resolved – even if you have dreamed about the same old spooky house for decades. Dream communication then also begins to evolve, and lucid dreaming becomes more regular as well.

Very, very cool indeed.

More Games To Exercise Your Genius

"Pushing Through The Threshold" Games

Most people are entrained to think that one single good idea in a lifetime is already a gift that only the chosen few will ever have any hope of receiving.

This is of course utter nonsense and we can generate as many new good ideas as we want to, once the energy mind comes online and starts to play with us.

Threshold games, especially if played in the right spirit, can blow these old limiting beliefs out of the water and delight you beyond measure.

In a threshold game, you don't ask for one good idea, but instead, for a dozen, or a hundred; and you'll be astonished to find that the magic generator of all things creative, your very own energy mind, will comply and send you as many as you want.

Other examples would be to ask for a set of 25 sculptures, 50 paintings, 14 songs for an album, 100 poems, or a dozen breakthrough ideas for your personal life or business.

I wanted to know if there really were no limits to this and asked for 365 exercises to help a person become more able to create wealth in their lives, one for every single day of the year, and none should take more than 60 seconds to read and not much longer than that to do on the spot.

I can tell you hand on heart that after the 365 wealth exercises[9] had been delivered, for month I was getting still more afterwards until it finally slowed down. If I needed any more convincing that there really is no end to the stream of ideas from the energy mind, that was it.

---

[9] The 60 Second Wealth Creators, DragonRising Publishing 2007

Try it for yourself. Keep the symbols face down, just draw one, and each time you will get what you ask for – it really doesn't stop.

This “creative limits buster” game is highly recommended for practice, and to update your self concept if you didn't know just what a creative genius you are equipped to be.

The Challenge Game

This is a good fun game to play with children or with friends at parties.

Here, another person draws or selects deliberately 3 symbols and you must tell the story of those symbols, immediately.

In a “quick fire” pattern where this happens very quickly back and forth, or around a table, you'll be amazed at the stories you get – and the practice you get at receiving “instant visions”.

Single Symbol Adventures

The simple Genius Symbols have worlds of potential and information behind them – we talk of these things as, for example, "weather, in its widest metaphorical sense".

Through the portal of the simple symbol "weather" you can travel to all manner of places, of times – you might remember something, an event that is just like a habitat, with a time, and a landscape, events happening there, and you can treat this memory exactly as though you were dealing with a habitat you just created.

If it is a disturbing memory, you can step right in, bring your friends and all your magic, stop time, rescue the aspect if it needs that, change things, make it into whatever you choose to make it into.

The portal "weather" can take you to very structural, high level places like thinking about the weather systems of Earth and how they influence – everything. We could go even higher and contemplate how the weather on Earth is influenced by sun storms and rays from outer space, and how those things are cosmic weather on a much grander scale.

Weather can lead you into the water cycle, or into the very heart of a single rain drop.

It could be that you think about the idea of emotions being like the weather and have thoughts and insights about that; or it could be that a habitat just unfolds you've never seen before and a story develops from there.

A single symbol adventure can be done open, like the example with the weather above and you can't know where it takes you; or you can put a set up on it and ask for one symbol that has particular relevance to a problem or a good situation you want to become even better still.

World Seed

A variant of the single symbol adventure is the World Seed.

Pick a symbol and let the entire habitat unfold around it and from there.

This is a particularly good way of playing with children and adults who might not be used entirely to Project Sanctuary, as "growing a world from seed" is quite natural and unfolds so happily, once you have the first (plant, animal, artefact, angel, person etc.) to get you started.

Simply keep asking non-leading questions such as, "What's behind the angel?" - "What happens next?" - "What else is there?" - "What else can you see/hear/sense/taste/scent/feel?" and after a little bit of digging to start with, soon enough, the story and the information will start to flow – and your vision is happening.

Negative Symbols

People are complex, but they are never, ever random. This game is very interesting indeed and can lead to some fascinating insights, messages from the dark side of the moon, as it were.

Get a piece of paper and jot down all 23 symbols, one after the other as they come to you. Do this quickly and do not number the symbols.

When you are happy that you have them all, count them.

Are there any symbols missing?

If yes, find the symbol or symbols that are missing on **this occasion.**

Take these symbols to give you a vision that is really important to you at this time to discover or resolve something you had not thought about at all, and/or not thought to ask about.

This is a fascinating exercise, especially if you do it quickly.

Even when the symbols are really well known to you later on, this will still work and give you some truly amazing insights from a very alternative perspective.

Playing The Game Without A Physical Set

Once you know the Genius Symbols, you can play without a set of physical markers or stones.

One simple way to play is to think about the Classic Game symbols in order (do you remember what they were? Can you do it now?).

Another way to play which is quite interesting is to take a large piece of paper and put one symbol at a time down, then write your impressions next to it.

This is very easy and something you can do at any time, anywhere, and it also allows you to read back the whole vision as it unfolded for you later on.

If you are playing with someone else, you can draw the symbols with a pen one at a time for them to see which is a good way of playing as well.

Into The Truly Unknown

"Show me something I have never seen before..."

I love that particular set up. It's like going to the cinema and finding a brand new movie that keeps you entertained and enthralled, but a whole lot better all around. Of course we do not need to restrict this to a visual modality.

"Let me have something I've never felt before."

"Send me something I have never heard before."

"Take me somewhere I have never been before..."

And if you really want to push it, you can ask for something that **no-one** has ever seen, heard, felt, experienced before...

Inventing Your Own Games

Of course, every single time you get out your personal Genius Symbol set, there lies the potential to develop your own games, your own ways to play, to play with patterns, grids, with sequences of revealing symbols, with using the symbols face down or face up, letting yourself be guided to the right movements and decisions in mind, body and spirit as you simply PLAY.

You will invent many spontaneous ways to play, especially if you start playing with others, in the hard or not, there is surprisingly little difference when all is said and done.

I strongly recommend that you keep your own symbol set nearby and just let yourself drift into play at random moments; to see them as you're passing by on your daily tasks and so you are inspired to pick a genius symbol or two, think about an event, vision or story, or come up with some new questions for the next real adventure.

THE GENIUS SYMBOLS IN SANCTUARY

I am an experienced Project Sanctuary player and it happened very naturally and just as soon as the symbols had been assembled, that I found myself in Pertineri Market, with a symbol set in front of me.

Visions Within Visions...

It is a fact that there are as many levels to this as you can consciously take; when you are starting from within a habitat, and then from there enter into another habitat – a vision within a vision - the habitats you visit and the visions you receive become more abstract, and the more levels you step away, the more abstract they become.

The ability of the conscious mind to stay in the game in spite of the rising levels of abstraction expands with practice; and you can get further and deeper into the game without the conscious mind "giving up the ghost," switching off, and you simply going unconscious or falling asleep.

We practically use this in a pattern from Project Sanctuary to be able to fall asleep at will – we enter into a sleep habitat, where we find a nice place to go to sleep. There, we dream another habitat, where again, we find a nice place to go to sleep in. There, we dream of another habitat, where again, we find a nice place, settle down, and go to sleep...

There are not many people in the world today who have ever managed more than five sleep habitats into this particular game without losing consciousness; if you play this correctly and go for full autogenic lucidity in every one, you too will find that there comes a time when the conscious mind can't go on any longer and it has to switch off.

Fascinating though this may be, the whole point of playing for visions and threshold shifts is of course that there is **lucidity**, with the energy mind and the conscious mind in harmony, because if the conscious mind isn't in the game, then "we" don't remember what happens and whatever has happened, might as well not exist at all for all the good it does!

If you find that difficult to conceptualise, imagine you dreamed up the cure for cancer one night, but when you woke up, you don't remember that you did...

That sort of thing is structurally entirely useless for practical every day life, as I said.

Playing one or two levels in, on the other hand, is a good practice pattern to expand the conscious mind's ability to "stay awake" and contributes greatly to our abilities to stay lucid, in waking life, in dreams, and in Sanctuary visions.

A First Genius Symbol Game In Sanctuary

Find a suitable habitat with a dwelling where you can play in peace, in protection, and to get the best possible results.

By all means, use this as a contract right here with the physical symbols to create this before you start. Once you have the habitat established, found your time and place in the data stream in other words, simply go there.

Find the place where the symbols are waiting for you, and sit yourself down just as you would in the hard.

Make a contract, just as you would in the hard; or have some friends present who can play with you, for you, or give suggestions about the contracts you might want to use here for a change.

Then, simply play the game as it unfolds, from there. Fascinating, and you can tell the difference in what kinds of visions you get when you play from within Sanctuary.

Playing On Behalf Of Others

When we play for ourselves, we are often given to making comparisons between the visions we have and our own life's memories; this is especially true for people who have been in therapy, or are therapists of some kind, but even for others, this is pretty unavoidable.

When we play on behalf of others, this is different.

We get visions that you can't track or trace as having anything whatsoever to do with you on any level; and that is fascinating and also I believe it to be especially enriching, as here we really get to add and touch **new and different data** of a kind that we have never had before.

In the hard, getting a steady stream of customers for Genius Symbol readings, coaching, teaching and visionary experiences is naturally limited by how much time you have to give; in Sanctuary, time and space are your oysters and you can take on as many astral clients as you want as well as making use of the width and infinity of choices beyond living people.

Streaming visions for an alien, a deceased loved one, a total stranger from a different time, for a friend even, is absolutely fascinating and represents a different set of skills to streaming visions on your own behalf and in response to your own questions and contracts.

Do remember that you are always playing for a threshold shift; in this case, not your own but that of your querent's.

Until and unless your querent is jumping with excitement and literally shouting, “Oh my!” - “Wow!” - “I got it!” - “Aha!” or “Eureka!” you're not done with the process.

It doesn't matter who your querent is, as well; even the most advanced, magical or otherwise wondrous entity underlies the rules of the Universe and they need to have their threshold shifts just the same as we do ☺

You, The Querent

A wonderful way to gain all sorts of new perspectives on the art of visioning, life, the universe and everything is for you to go and get a vision from someone else.

This someone else could be anyone, of course – but who should it be for you on this occasion?

A famous seer from way back when?

An aspect of your self who could do with the practice?

One of your friends?

You, yourself as you are right now?

A wiser version of you from the future?

Or a more connected child version of you from the past?

An alien who will catalyse the game on your behalf?

This is endlessly fascinating, and your own responses to the game and as it progresses from this perspective is also something quite priceless, and a unique experience in its own right.

Living Symbol Experiences

The Genius Symbols are portals, as we have noted; in Sanctuary, you can make this quite real and literal.

You might like to try a game whereby you visit a building or a structure with 23 doors, and each one has one of the symbols on it or over it – just know that when you step through that portal, you will enter into a new habitat that will bring you closer to understanding the symbol or your relationship with it.

This is a very fascinating experience indeed and will offer many adventures in its own right; as nothing is ever "finished", you can also take many trips through the same portal and learn something new, **evolve yourself further**, every time in a spiral movement of unfoldment that never ends, as long as you live.

Exciting, exciting, exciting!

Symbols & Artefacts

Making artefacts out of the symbols, or decorating artefacts with the symbols in Sanctuary is also a truly fascinating endeavour.

Imagine a sword and it has the time symbol engraved in the blade!

Oh my!

What **could** you do with that?

What might you use it for?

Where would that come in handy? Or... when...?

Or perhaps a cup with the symbol for stardust...?

A fruit and on closer inspection, it has the gift symbol in its very structure...?

A tree and every leaf carries the symbol of the dance...?

This is a truly delightful game, and one I hope you will allow yourself to play and experience in full.

Children & The Genius Symbols

Children love Project Sanctuary and they are natural players. They can show adults up sincerely in how easily they take to it, and how trouble free they simply dive into the stories and find outstanding resolutions.

You can play with children in the hard, and you can also play with Sanctuary children – with your magical child within, with child aspects, and with other kinds of Sanctuary children, including in Soul Piloting.

You can play the entire game in Sanctuary or you can have the child you're playing with come to you whilst you play with the symbols in the hard.

There are three main ways in which you can play with children.

One is to tell them a story; the second, to have them tell you a story, and the third is to create a story together.

None of these is "better" or inherently more beneficial than any of the others; if you are playing with children, you should do all three because they are very different and actualise different aspects of us, the child/ren and the relationship that exists between you.

A First Symbol Experience

I personally like to just show the symbols to a child on the first time out and let the child tell me and show me what needs to happen next.

Usually, children find the symbols on the templates/stones quite fascinating and will ask questions or tell you things; if you follow on with that, you can't go far wrong.

You can tell a child about the symbols and what they mean, but don't bore the kid to tears with too much detail.

I like to let the child show me which symbols they find most interesting and just let something develop from there.

At some point, I will offer a First Sanctuary experience. To have a world of their own is something children really like; and just like with adults, it gets the flow going, is good fun to do and practises the basic skills you need to become a great player as a by-the-by and while you're doing it.

A First Story Experience

Depending on the child and whether you choose the option of you telling the story, the child telling the story or both of you creating the story between you, it's a good idea to get a first story going so the child gets the idea that Project Sanctuary is an active place where you get to have great adventures.

Asking the child, "What kind of story should we make today?" will produce a contract, just as simple as that and right away.

When you do play with children, the way they immediately come out with what they want, and their excitement about "A story about robots and spaceships and lots of aliens!" can teach you where you may have been stodgy and boring when you were asking for your own games to play.

You can start with the Classic Game symbols and trust me, things will just follow on from there.

Giving & Receiving Gifts

The Gift is an original Project Sanctuary pattern whereby an energy form is created and sent to a recipient as "your special gift for them, something that only you have the power to give".

This is a practice exercise for Project Sanctuary because it is the energy mind which has to create and send The Gift; consciously, we can't know how to do either, as usual.

"Let's send the perfect gift to Aunty Mary to help her not be so sad any more. What shall it be?"

You can draw a random symbol and base your gift on that; you can also create a complete habitat and look for the gift inside of it.

When we have The Gift, we send it out with a gesture like you would set free a bird you hold in your hands, so it can fly away and find its recipient.

Giving The Gift is a wonderfully empowering and moving experience that has magical results in the hard as well; it is a piece of magic that anyone can do and that is quite real.

Gifts can be given to anyone and anything, so one can send a gift to a pet, to the environment, to a business, to a situation, and it will always improve the atmosphere and make things brighter.

Receiving The Gift, on the other hand, can be a little bit more tricky.

Ask a friend for a The Gift and see what happens next; this is a wonderful opportunity to "get something" that is needed and wanted, and probably structurally important for health, well-being and evolution.

How this gift is integrated is of the essence here.

Where does the gift fit, where does it belong, what are we to DO with it?

If you are given a book on birds, are you supposed to say "Thanks a lot!" and then just leave it on a shelf?

In the Sanctuary realms, we do a whole lot more than that.

You have to remember to think magically – especially when The Gifts are concerned.

The book on birds is crying out to be taken somewhere, opened up and all the birds on the colour pictures come to life, fly out of the pages of the book and start to sing in the tree tops; the book itself turns into a big brown owl who might become a friend perhaps...

Think of receiving a The Gift as a puzzle in its own right and find where it needs to go, what it needs to do, how it needs to be received.

It's a skill set that is very valuable, and soon learned, even by the youngest children, and something that will stand them in good stead throughout life, opening the doors for these children to be able to receive miracles, when they come their way.

Bedtime Stories & Meta Stories

Not all stories conclude within minutes; and many of those stories which do are an entrance into that world and it is possible to have many instalments, or even a fully fledged meta story.

Project Sanctuary bedtime stories are simply vastly superior to looking at a picture book someone else has written in every way possible.

The stories are going to be spot on appropriate to delight the child; if you ask in your contract for a story that will give the child good dreams and make it sleep deeply, rest amazingly and wake up bright and fully refreshed, you'll be doing a grand job.

There are many other concerns, hopes and dreams you may have for the child you can build into the contract – especially the issues of that day make for a good set up to be resolved and evolved through a story.

Even if you have played with the symbols only a few times, you'll soon be able to not need to look at the stones any longer but see them in your mind instead; and so you can sit in the dark with your child and create a world that both of you can see, an intense rapport that is very precious but also incredibly educational for the child in question.

Once a story is under way, the child can pick up their power and help change and morph it more to their liking; again, this is VASTLY superior to being just a recipient for a story that is locked down in black and white letters on a page by a third party who isn't even in the room.

If the story gets stuck at any time, you can call on the Genius Symbols to come to your aid and suggest something to help you move the story along and to a very successful and delightful result and effect.

This is pure magic, and it also makes the child respect you in a whole new way as you are the story teller, not just a reader for someone who is cleverer and somewhere far away.

The same works in reverse as the story teller begins to appreciate the intelligence and creativity of their child in a whole new way, and the depth of rapport and connection achieved resonates out from these experiences far and wide into other places.

Your special stories will remain a source of connection and also a place you can return to in the future in case this should be required, or bad things happen, to re-affirm this special magical connection through the worlds you created between you.

This is truly magical, and the long term repercussions of making these sort of connections with a child should not be underestimated.

They may well last beyond even the end of life.

Stories & Pictures

Making a picture from a Project Sanctuary story is also a wonderful thing to do on a rainy afternoon, or at any time you're up for a deeply connective and sharing experience with a child.

Instead of just telling the story, you, the child or both of you together get to paint the time of year, the landscape, the weather, the dwelling, the friends, the artefacts.

This can be one picture, or a whole series of pictures; it can also be just simple cartoon like jottings on a piece of paper as well as full colour creations to hang on the wall.

Making a story, a habitat or a special threshold shift moment hard and visibly manifest in the hard like that is a very magical thing to do, and both the process, as well as the results, represent truly superior learning.

Little Worlds

Something that I have always enjoyed tremendously and which children absolutely love is to build “a little world” in miniature.

You can build a world on a dinner plate, or in the garden; on the beach or in a shoe box; or make a larger world so the child can use their play figures or toy animals as a part of this world.

A little sand, a few sticks and twigs for big stately trees, a little silver foil for a lake and a pebble for a mountain, and you're up and away.

Making little worlds and playing games in these is just fabulous. You really don't need much in the way of equipment, and it's tremendous fun.

Of course, if you want to go to town and make models of castles and use big crystals for alien worlds and such, by all means!

This is truly one of my favourite “children's games” of all time.

Soul Piloting for Children

Children often feel useless and pointless in today's societies.

Soul Pilot work – to offer one's services to save lost souls - does significantly improve a person's sense of worth and self esteem, and a child is no different in that respect to anyone else.

Each child has its own unique vibration and will attract its own unique claimants; these will be different from yours and completely unique to the child themselves.

That in and of itself is a revelation to most children, that it is they who are needed here absolutely, and that you are only here to advise – the claimant is their own.

Start with a basic classic lay out, but create the contract that the child wants to help someone who needs their help today by placing the spirit symbol at the front of the lay out.

Make sure you don't overwhelm the child or try and take the lead, no matter how much you want to – remember, this is the child's claimant and you are only there in an advisory role, serving as the child's "friend" on this occasion.

And you know how a real friend helps you – definitely not by taking the game away from you and playing it in your stead!

Dreams & Nightmares

Children are very close to their dreams, in a way we have quite forgotten what that's like. Talking to a child about their dreams is a very good thing to do in the first place, but to take any dreams into Sanctuary to explore them further or to resolve them in a different way in the case of nightmares, is an astonishing thing to teach to a young child.

Do bear in mind with all these things that when we are playing Project Sanctuary with a child, this is not an entertainment like reading out a book that you have to do over and over and over again until you're sick to death of it – the child is learning how to do things with their own minds instead.

Once you've done a few dream resolutions with your child, they can do this themselves at any time when they need to; **that is a life skill** and something no-one can ever take away from them again.

It is nice to offer the opportunity to work through something with you by their side if that's necessary; but you will find that children soon make Sanctuary their own and will surprise you with what they are doing there – and most likely, inspire you to try new things and become more flexible and exciting in your adventures.

I would also add that if you were to bring one of your own bad dreams to the table, as an equal in the game, and ask for the child's help in the game of dream resolution, something honest, magical and deeply aligning takes place between two human beings, regardless of the labels they carry in society.

Games for Older Children & Teenagers

It might be thought that older children, adolescent boys and stroppy teenagers would be resistant to playing Project Sanctuary with their elders or progenitors, but you'd be wrong about that.

Let's not forget that you can play Project Sanctuary for sex, for example, and that someone who knows how to make a basic habitat and get autogenic there will then also have the ability to invite any pop star, sports hero or other desired personage there and have some jolly good fun – and all nice and clean without the risk of STDs or pregnancy!

Project Sanctuary isn't daydreaming, and whatever is important to your youngster, be it being more popular at school, being better at sports, getting a date with a pop idol, battling dragons, exploring alien planets, saving polar bears or getting married to the boy next door and living happily ever after, can be played as a Sanctuary game – and it will have an evolutionary effect on the person who is playing that.

The ability to "step into" and become a part of something they find fascinating, from a computer game to a TV show, a movie or a Manga comic, a story from history or a favourite book, is a highly attractive proposition and one that is going to strongly motivate an older child to have a go with Project Sanctuary, especially on their own and in the privacy of their own minds.

- **Remember that Project Sanctuary is a LIFE SKILL.**

It affords the player a platform to satisfy themselves in a different way, try out many different things, situations, people, behaviours, movements, skills and the rest in a safe and supportive environment. It allows us to practice and rehearse behaviour that will stand up to the hard when it comes to it because it is autogenic and very close, if not indistinguishable from, actual hard learning and experience.

All youngsters and teenagers day dream; to turn this into real autogenic fantasy that is under their own control and that they can use to further their aims, hopes and dreams of this life is once again, totally priceless.

If you explain this a little, tell a story or two, and invite them to try just the basic "First Sanctuary" for themselves, you'll be doing your children a favour that will earn you a lifetime's gratitude all by itself.

Bringing Project Sanctuary Into The Family

My children and my loved ones know who my Sanctuary friends are. They know their names and even enquire every so often about their well being, or if there's any interesting news, much as you would enquire about an uncle who lives in Alaska.

Project Sanctuary is a part of my family.

We have shared experiences, shared habitats we can refer to; on long car journeys, we may play a bit of Project Sanctuary and we also employ Project Sanctuary style resolutions to many hard situations as a matter of fact.

Referring to someone's room as their habitat, for example, isn't just fun but also very meaningful on many different levels.

Well, do you have dirty socks strewn about on the floor of your dwelling in your sanctuary?

I guess not... ☺

Project Sanctuary adds totally different dimensions to conversations you can have with your spouse, your children, your friends in the hard.

It is like whatever we get out of watching soap operas is happening for real and on a personal basis.

Having a person around of whom you know that they are currently on a quest to retrieve a king's sword from the Northern Mountains as well as whatever else they're doing – going to work, doing the gardening, clearing out the garage etc. - makes that person simply much more **interesting.**

More multi-faceted, more rich, more deep, more exciting to be with, and you have that wondrous factor of evolution and forward movement built in by default.

That person will change when they have had their threshold shift in the story – that will make them new, and even more exciting than they were before.

More experienced, more intelligent, more reasonable, more centred, more self controlled, probably more compassionate and understanding as well – how cool!

- **We're living with interesting people who are evolving.**

We have a platform to talk about hopes and dreams, as well as bills and whose turn it is to clean the toilets.

That's a fabulous thing to have in your family life and I can tell you that it hasn't made any of us less "reality orientated" but in fact, far more so – because when delusion and illusion and day dreaming stops, real imagination and creativity enters and then the world comes alive with mystery, magic and extraordinary potential.

More About The Genius Symbols

Symbol Meditations

A meditation is just being mindful and thinking about something in depth, putting your full attention and focus there and not anywhere else for a time.

There is no need for hypnosis, drums and incense; and neither is there any need for lying down with crystals on your chakras in order to meditate on anything.

Call it "musing" on something for that is in essence what we do.

With the symbols, it is easy to help you focus on something by holding the symbol in your hand and just looking at it.

In this chapter, I would like to share some interesting ideas for meditations, explorations, adventures and experiences you can try out for yourself, even if only really briefly whilst you're having a cup of coffee, that can be really quite valuable.

Gift VS Trade

Here is an example of using two symbols to get balance and clarity on a topic that is quite important for daily life. This is a particular example, but you can use this pattern on any of the topics that the symbols represent and where there may be confusion or conflict.

In this example, I have noted with great interest that people do get their Gifts and Trades mixed up.

- **A gift is unconditional and NOTHING is required back in return; a trade is a trade where something is EXCHANGED.**

Hold the symbols for gift and trade in each hand and tune into their different energies, how they feel, what connotations they have for you; if you are an EmoTrance practitioner, of course you might like to "flow" the respective energies through you so that you are clear on how they feel, and what they are.

At some point, switch hands and thus gain another perspective; if you feel you need further help, run a Gift and a Trade story to get further information and insight into not just how they differ and how they work, but also on YOUR unique perspective because of your life's experiences and how that affects the way the symbols work for you and what they mean.

Symbol Of The Day

Keep your symbol set somewhere where it is out in the open and as you pass by on your daily life, pick a symbol – pick any symbol.

That's your "symbol of the day" - something for you to think about as you go through your daily life, here and there, nothing major, just keep it in the back of your mind, see if anything interesting happens or pops up in relation to the symbol of the day.

The people who tried this in the testing phase said to a man (and a woman, of course) that they enjoyed this especially and it helped them "bring the worlds closer together".

What is particularly interesting is that when after a time you get the same symbol, you can really notice how much you have moved on from the last time you thought about it.

You notice your evolution and your progress as far as both understanding these concepts and how they work is concerned, but also how you are now using these understandings to make improvements in your very practical, daily life.

Excellent exercise.

Daily Quick Meditation

At any time you like, during a coffee break, before you go to bed, or first thing in the morning, draw a symbol or deliberately choose a symbol and have a moment to hold it, feel it, think about it, and perhaps even make some choices and decisions relating to that.

You might pick the house symbol on one occasion and take this as an impetus to clean out your bedroom, for example.

The beauty of the Genius Symbols is that because they are so multi-dimensional, they can be a doorway to THE most mundane of activities as well as the most esoteric and far out journeys of consciousness possible.

You are in total control of what you want to do, and where you want to go at any given time – including being in control enough to give up your control to the energy mind and ask for something that you don't know what it might be, and that could be anything at all. ☺

EmoTrance Symbol Exercises

This is a very, very interesting way of learning and changing not just your mind, but your entire energy system using the energy of the symbols.

We have already talked about using the EmoTrance[10] method to clear blockages and remove shields to symbols; but you can take this much, much further.

For example:

Pick a symbol, hold in your hand, and tune into the energy of it. Remember that the symbol isn't a static rock with a little picture painted on it, but in energetic terms, that it is a portal that streams information through it.

Let this information, this unique energy enter into your body.

Where is this energy entering your body?

Track and trace the energy flow all the way in, through and out your body.

Smooth any rough spots, heal any disturbances along the way, remove blockages – soften and flow! - and keep running this energy until you reach the energized end state[11].

When you are done, sit down for a moment and take time to reflect on how you have changed your mind, what new things you have learned, or how previous assessments have changed in the light of this new experience.

That's a pretty priceless form of self help and a unique experience with every one of these symbols.

---

[10] Oceans Of Energy, DragonRising 2003

[11] The "energized end state" is the EmoTrance word for a threshold shift having occurred and a person is delighted, energized, buzzing, and excited about their "Eureka!" experience.

You can also use EmoTrance to take in the energy of an entire story spread, a pattern, a complete unfoldment and a whole symbol sphere; and of course using EmoTrance to track disturbances while you are playing the story, becoming aware of your responses and not just playing for a threshold shift, but a threshold shift that is also an energized end state, is pretty amazing.

Once you have experienced the energy of the symbols in this way, you can then channel the energy of a symbol at any time you choose.

To begin with, draw the symbol in the air in front of you to help you tune into that particular energy form, then channel it through your body.

Once you can feel the threshold shift, you have evoked that energy form and now you can act and use that state for the purpose you want.

Just for interest, have a thought where you might find it useful to channel the energy of fountain, the gift, stardust, time, space, and alien.

Quite fascinating and the uses of this are as are all things in the realms of energy and Sanctuary, probably infinite.

Using The Symbols In Daily Life

Can you use the time symbol on your alarm clock so you stop being constantly late?

Can you have a piece of jewellery made for you that features the magic symbol?

Can you draw a gift symbol on a birthday card beneath your name?

Can you draw the dragon wings symbol on a project folder to help you keep the "bigger picture" and not get lost in the details?

Can you draw the angel symbol in the air before you with both hands to invite that energy into your life?

Can you decorate a cake with stardust, the light and the dance?

Can you evoke a fountain in your living room?

Yes, of course you can.

Indeed I would encourage the use of the symbols at any time you need help from the "powers that be".

The Project Sanctuary Genius Symbols are universal and once they are known to you and to your energy mind, you can use them to communicate in many different ways indeed.

The symbols are the simple shapes they are for a reason, and that reason is that they are easy to replicate in movements.

You can use hand movements to evoke the symbols, there does not have to be a pen involved. You can draw them using your fingertips into the sand, or invisibly onto a surface, object, or even a person if you feel that would help.

In fact, the more you make these symbols a part of your life, the more powerful they become as portals of communication for you. You will find many other uses arising spontaneously as and when it is needed; this is a very wonderful thing, and a very powerful one on many different levels.

Blessings & Problem Help

At one time, I had just finished a reading for someone and was still sitting with the symbols spread out before me.

I didn't have the time for a story so it occurred to me to go through the symbols one by one and just thank the universe at large for the blessings I have in my life.

I picked up one symbol after the other and thanked for the time I've been given, and the good times; the space of freedom I have; my outstanding friends, the wonderful people in my life, my animal friends, past and present and so forth until every symbol had transmitted my gratitude.

That was such a lovely and uplifting thing to do, I wanted to share it with you and encourage you to try that for a change.

On another occasion, I used the same pattern of taking one idea and using the symbols to touch many aspects of that for problem solving.

How does space come into this problem? What can time do to help? What ideas do the friends have?

After just two or three symbols, you already feel the shift and the lifting, the new ideas coming in from all directions; but if you keep going and do all 23, you'll have even more fun – and I promise you, you will never ever think about that problem in the same way again.

Another use of the same pattern I employed one day was to state what I wanted on each symbol, to use it as a kind of shopping list for Father Christmas, or rather the powers that be, to let them know what I wanted in my life, what I felt was missing, what I found troubling and wanted resolution for.

This was a very interesting and freeing exercise, and to my surprise (although why I should be surprised by that, I really don't know, after all I been through!) some of the things I said I wanted began to come to pass pretty much immediately.

This basic pattern of using the symbols to aspect all 23 back on one single (idea, problem, set up, story, event, person, etc.) gives you an amazing depth of richness on your start up (idea, problem, set up, story, person etc.)

It puts so much information together, from so many different levels, and then aligns it all to create this whole new reality that emerges, it's truly amazing each and every time you do this.

Try it on a memory or event in your life that you think was formative or particularly disturbing or destructive, trauma or Guiding Star, it matters not.

You don't just get one new perspective out of it, but a whole new world of possibilities, information, and resolutions.

The Spirit Of The Symbols

At the very highest level, there is a spirit of the symbol behind each one.

The spirit of the land, the spirit of animals, the spirit of the light – these are not gods but they are existences in the Universe with very different and distinct attributes, each one.

We human beings relate best when we personalise things and treat them as though they were human-like; that's the way we are wired naturally as social animals.

If you can handle the fact that this is so, yet remain logical enough not to slide off and confuse the symbols with some sort of higher beings, which they are not, you can use a personal approach to working with the Genius Symbols which is human and both beautiful as well as powerful.

You can address the spirit of time, or the lord of time, in a personal fashion and have conversations with it, request things from it, tell it things, make friends with it.

How would your life be different if time itself was on your side, was your friend, loved you and you would love time in return?

Of course, you would have a much better "attitude" to time, a completely different approach to solving problems relating to time and how you handle time, and a great many conflicts that you currently have with time management would simply disappear.

This is one example of 23 where a close, very personal relationship with the spirit of the symbol can be of practical use in daily life.

It goes further than that.

The human propensity to relate to other occurrences as though they had human qualities allows one to use the Genius Symbols for all manner of things we can't use humans for.

We can ask them for advice in a personal fashion; and one pattern I observed spontaneously was to ask the symbols for forgiveness.

That may sound really strange, but the person in question apologized sincerely and most heartfelt for all their transgressions against the spirit of time, space, plants, animals, people, spirits, the light and so forth; and I have rarely seen such powerful energy work in action.

Another place where I have observed a similarly powerful effect was someone calling in the spirit of X when faced with a difficult and overwhelming situation.

This must be very similar process that is used in various religious practices by calling on a variety of deities, saints or spirits that have humanized features and names; it is clearly a natural behaviour for humans and it works. The symbols have the advantage that they are clean and clearly just symbols; and we can evoke their energy without getting entangled in believing that these are people, or anything even remotely like people, which is the danger when such symbols become too human-like, as would be the case if we turned the Lord of the Animals into a humanoid being and started to worship it.

The Genius Symbols can function as a structural personal pantheon that is free from religion and does not conflict with religion.

Essentially, the symbols are descriptions of 23 universal and existing energy forms which we can relate to in many different ways.

The more personal we can make this relationship, the more helpful these energy forms can be; and this is additional to the bridging function the symbols perform for connecting the energy mind to the conscious mind, and a unique feature of the Genius Symbols in and of themselves.

More Symbols, Different Symbols

Please understand that the Project Sanctuary Genius Symbols are not like a deck of Tarot cards – they are not carved in stone by "someone else who knows better" to remain like that forever.

I do believe the problem with most magical systems has always been that they originally evolved out of their own time and space context, but then the context became lost in time as people moved on, energetically, mentally, societally and so the chasm between the users and the old fashioned symbols just grew and grew to the point where many magical systems just don't make sense to us today any longer because we are not correctly interpreting or understanding the meanings and metaphors that were once known to everyone in that society.

Your own or a child's slightly wonky stick figure drawn on a piece of rock is immensely more magical than someone else's incredibly expensive set of works of clever art.

More magical to you. More personal to you. More directly linked with you and thereby easier to use, more approachable and much more under your own control because you understand how it works.

Thereby, I encourage you absolutely to evolve the symbols for your own personal use.

You might want to use more symbols or slightly different ones than the ones I am proposing here.

You can absolutely change the shapes of the symbols if you want to.

- **THE ACT OF DRAWING A SYMBOL IS A HUMAN RIGHT.**

It is your birthright.

Life, liberty, the pursuit of happiness and to draw any symbol you like for any reason, at any time in your life.

You can also change your mind on certain symbols; I certainly reserve that right as well as I live, learn and grow and through the very practice of using the symbols find out much more about how these things affect me, my stories, and my visions.

The symbol set of 23 I have proposed here is a starting point, something to get us going, something so we can write brand new stories for tomorrow – which will then be the jump off point into a whole new time, and presumably, other and even better Genius Symbols.

One thing I would ask of you however.

- **Be mindful of the symbols.**

Keep it simple.

Try and keep even personal symbols so that others can also read them, also understand them – without the need of a hundred years in "magic school" to try and make sense of your idiosyncratic convoluted processes!

That is really important as we try and regroup to a place where magic is easy and natural and this is the one place where I do believe past generations have lost the plot on so many occasions.

Even though nature is incredibly complex and multi-layered, it is also on another level, very simple; there is a big difference between "complex" and "complicated".

In the past people thought erroneously that if you split up nature into separate parts and study all the bits separately, you will eventually "know it all" but that truly doesn't work and is simply wrong.

A symbol set of 1,436 symbols, one for every occasional detail, that has to be studied for decades is **useless**.

It is useless, it is pointless, and the decades of study are a horrendous waste of time during which a person could have amassed so much knowledge and wisdom if they'd played it straight from the start, the loss of life would be veritably shocking.

As an example, splitting up the people symbol into fair haired maidens, red haired maidens, brown haired maidens, the occasional albino maiden, black haired maidens with curly hair, black haired maidens with straight hair, young women who aren't maidens any more but not middle aged yet with curly blond hair, boys under the age of 3 with brown skins, men over 6' 4" from a Northern country and so on, on, on, on, on ad infinitum serves no purpose whatsoever.

The energy mind will tell you EXACTLY what kind of person you are dealing with the instant you put your fingertip on the people symbol in the story or vision you are playing.

There really is no need for separate symbols for men and women, children and old people and so forth.

Not only does this approach destroy the inherent infinite possibilities of the direct vision which tells you clearly about one single individual who is entirely unique in all times spent as you are trying to stuff this individual into one of however many categories you have made for yourself and the fit is at best bearable but never ever perfect or ever really right; not only does this multi-category approach make it nearly impossible for a person to enter into the game swiftly and without years of all sorts of wasted study; but also it destroys the bigger picture – hey, my friend, and no matter who or what you've just seen, they are a person.

The people symbol reminds us of that and keeps us steady in a place where we cannot afford to get either sentimental, or judgemental, or freaked out, or turned on, or any of the many "human reactions" we would normally accord to a "category within" humanity, such as victim, or abuser, or sex object or madonna.

The current propensity to pull things apart to try and make sense of them, when the sense of these things can **ONLY BE KNOWN IF THE CONTEXT IS KNOWN,** has in truth been the greatest bedevilment of science, art and religion alike.

When you come to make or add your own symbols, please be wise.

If you don't like a symbol, meditate on it for a while. There may be a good reason why you are having a negative reaction to it, and by clearing that negative reaction (including "I don't need that symbol at all! I'll just delete it ..") you will advance in your own personal development and understanding.

If you have meditated on it and you REALLY don't need that symbol, then take it out. Keep it tight, keep it neat and don't add anything that isn't strictly necessary, or where the purpose is already achieved in one of the other symbols, only you hadn't noticed that at first.

When you are adding a new symbol, hold it up against all the existing ones and feel if there is indeed, enough of a structural difference to make it a doorway to a whole domain of levels and layers in its own right.

Do we really need a little car as a symbol for travel?

Or is that not already a major function of the space symbol in all ways?

At the end of the day, they're your symbols.

You do as you please with them.

Create them, re-create them, change them.

Know that you can always change your mind and take a symbol back, or drop it if it doesn't serve your purposes or turns out to have been a misunderstanding. Be mindful, pay attention, do things honestly and I can't see how you could possibly go wrong with this, so by all means – **just play.**

Questions & Answers

How do I know it's really a vision and not a fantasy or day dream?

You can <u>feel</u> the difference. You can feel it on many levels, but most of all, you feel it when the threshold shifts happen. Day dreams don't give you a rush of excitement, lots of new ideas, insights and extra energy to put what you've learned into practice.

Also, I always find that the real visions are MOVING. They are resonant, alive, full of energy and I respond to that with having feelings and sensations. I can be shocked, overjoyed, happy, sigh with delicious relief and all sorts.

One last pointer that you're having a real vision is when you are simply surprised by what happens. If you are surprised, then "you" didn't know, and you didn't "make it up".

Best advice for you is to stop worrying and start playing. Take some time establishing your First Sanctuary and playing in those realms in any way you choose. That's where you learn the basics as you play.

Are you supposed to play with eyes open, or eyes shut?

That is a very good question, and I strongly recommend you play "eyes open" and focused on the symbol to start with and until you know what you're doing.

One of the biggest problems and blockages that people have with "visions" is that they expect to see them through their "eyes of day", the physical eyes. There are certain neurological pathways that lead to our eyes of day; and they are NOT THE SAME PATHWAYS you travel on for visions, not at all!

So if you're trying to see something, and you are unwittingly instructing your consciousness to travel to the eyes of day, you'll get nothing visionary; and when your eyes are closed, you get all sorts of confusion happening.

When you focus your eyes on the symbol, you stop yourself from accessing all sorts of things - memories, ideas, pictures seen, here, there everywhere in a big jumble! - and the eyes of day are kept busy with looking at the symbol.

That's when your energy mind has a chance to send you information, visions in that OTHER way - things we are used to calling thoughts or ideas, sensations, sounds, feelings, intuitions.

That's where the INFORMATION for the vision comes from.

So until and unless you have learned that you don't travel to your eyes to see with those when you are wanting to experience a vision, keep your eyes open and focused on the symbol. That will work perfectly for you.

> ***Do you have to get into an altered state of consciousness first in order to use the Genius Symbols? And how do you do that?***

One of the features of working with Project Sanctuary in general and the Genius Symbols in particular I am the most proud of is that you do not have to learn to meditate, self hypnotise, or roll back your eyes and be taken over by spirits before you can start to work with the data stream of the energy mind.

There is no need whatsoever to do any form of altering your consciousness for using the symbols. This happens as a by-the-by when you move your consciousness into those realms by going into the habitat where the events of the vision take place.

Which is perfect because you can start at any time, anywhere, and at will.

> ***I find it difficult to keep concentration, every little sound or disturbances bounces me out of the vision and that happens all the time?***

The more stressed you are, the more you bounce out of anything at the slightest creak or tweak; stress makes you jumpy and unable to hold your focus.

Give yourself some time to relax down (there is some good advice on that at the beginning of this book) and importantly, don't wind yourself up by having a negative attitude to yourself or allowing yourself to get frustrated too quickly.

Every time you bounce out, stay calm, say out aloud, "Where were we? What was the last thing I remember? I was trying to figure out what the weather was like on that afternoon in Winter..."

After the first few attempts, you will find that as soon as you say, "Where were we?" you flash right back to where you were just as quickly as you bounced out when there was a disturbance.

If you keep calm and keep calmly re-directing your attention by asking yourself relevant questions out aloud, eventually a form of submission occurs and the stories, memories and visions become steady, then extremely resonant and real.

It's a practice matter but also always a question of how stressed you are when you are doing this. Luckily, when you really engage in working with your attention and your energy mind, that is in and of itself a far greater de-stressor than most other things, so you enter a virtuous spiral soon enough.

I have some thoughts and ideas but they don't seem very real?

Pick any thought or idea and describe it in detail. The more detail you add, the more real things become until there is a threshold shift and it's all there, really real, like a lucid dream.

Remember to **ask out aloud and answer out aloud** as well. That really helps at the beginning. Then you can switch to answering and asking loudly in your mind instead, and eventually you can do that thing where you pay attention to the details of sight, sound, scent, taste, feel, and touch right away and as a matter of fact.

What do you do if you get a scary vision?

You evolve it. Find the point/s of leverage and move it on towards a threshold shift, that's what we mean by evolving it. Remember you have all the magic of all the worlds and then some; so if you get a scary vision of thousands of evil creatures invading a house where your loved ones are hiding out, you can do whatever you like to find a resolution - taking the house away, transporting your loved ones away, negotiating, or even changing the nature of the evil creatures so they are no longer a threat.

Using the dragon wings symbol to take you up to see the bigger picture as soon as possible will help as well not to get swept up in a scary vision, the friends symbol brings you helpful friends, and the magic symbol reminds you that all of this is only energy.

But for what it's worth, as you are co-operating with your energy mind and with the set ups for Project Sanctuary in general, you won't get one unless you ask, and even then, it will be perfectly in keeping with your ability to solve it, or at least, evolve it.

I got a story but I don't understand what it means or what it has to do with my question/contract.

That usually happens if you haven't played far enough to get a threshold shift. Remember the threshold shift is that moment when you go, "Eureka!!!" and it all becomes clear to you in a lightning strike type flash you can feel in your physical body. That's when you understand what the story was all about and how it relates to your question and the contract. Do remember also you can ask your friends for further clarification, or use extra symbols to "shed more light" on the situation.

Sometimes, the energy mind doesn't understand that we don't understand. I have had occasions where I simply sat down in the story and refused to go any further until something changed, something different happened. In the story, I sat there for nearly a year; in real time, it was about one second before my energy mind got it and sent me further information that re-started the story and finally (after another three minutes!) brought it to a very satisfying conclusion.

Don't stop until you get your threshold shift!

Why are there no bad symbols to warn you of danger?

There are many reasons why there are no bad symbols, only neutral symbols that are about information – energy, in other words.

The first reason is that there is no good and bad energy, only energy; just as there are no good or bad raindrops in nature. To understand the world, we have to stop judging things in terms of black and white and get with the program – which is fluent, interactive, and always evolving.

The second reason is that no matter how often the tarot reader tries to explain to a person that getting the death card is a "good" thing, people get terrified by "bad" symbols, and as soon as a person gets to be terrified, they lose their logic, their reasoning, and access to their energy mind on top of that. Nothing good can come of it at any level, plus it makes a person even less likely to work with the energy mind if they are constantly terrified of learning something terrifying each time they play.

The third reason is that if something needs to be known or a danger needs to be brought into conscious awareness, of course our visions will express that to us clearly. If you pick up the plant symbol and you see wilted roses as your vision, that tells you all you need to know about what that the energy mind had to say about your contract or question. We have been warned but without having to now live in fear of the plant symbol the next time we use the Genius Symbols.

Help! I'm having visions and getting stories but they're neither properly lucid or completely autogenic!

Take it easy! You get better with practice. and look at it this way. So you **are getting some stories and visions.**

Do you know how many people on this planet don't? Never do? Not ever? Don't know how?

Do you know how truly wondrous it is that you are being given stories by your energy mind that you can receive?

Jump for joy and keep practising.

What also helps tremendously is to use the symbols themselves to help you repair and improve your own systems.

I thought I was pretty good at having visions - until the day I played a game to "improve my magic" and found out that I could have much better visions! and now I do.

Play a game for, "Give me some thing that will improve my ability to experience the visions in autogenic lucidity!" or whatever words you want to choose.

Go for the threshold shift, and take it from there.

I found a story - but now, it won't stop! It's been going on for days and there is no end in sight!

Ah... yes. We call this a "meta story".

Wuthering Heights, Lord of The Rings, Harry Potter, Star Wars - those are examples of meta stories, stories or visions that take on a life of their own and rush like a river through the events that unfold.

I - and everyone else I've ever known who has played a real meta story of their own - consider myself extremely blessed to have been given one a huge privilege and an honour.

I also personally feel that a good meta story of your own is about the most fun you can have with your clothes on.

Meta stories are always extremely valuable and transformational to an individual, and after a short time, you learn to manage them and your ordinary daily activities, side by side.

Eventually, the meta story will resolve or come to an end; I think these stories aren't about a single threshold shift, but represent a real journey of some kind, with many, many threshold shifts along the way.

If you have found a meta story, or rather, if it has found you, enjoy it for all its worth. It's a very precious, very special experience indeed.

Do I really have to go through the trouble of making a symbol set? Can't I just play in my head?

Ah, you're one like me, I can tell. I did that for a while and finally gave in and painted the symbols on beach pebbles.

I'm by default the most experienced Project Sanctuary player in the world, and I can tell you that to hold, touch and look at the 3D physical stones/objects with the symbols painted on them improved MY visions and my ability to hold the focus, play quickly, get astonishing shifts and open up new doors I didn't even know were there before.

If that is so for me then I would say, yes.

There's merit in "taking the time and trouble" to make your own symbol set, to look at, to hold in your hands, to engage your entire person, mind, body, energy mind altogether and at the same time.

Remember, the reward is to be a real visionary genius – that's worth the trouble of finding a few pebbles, don't you think?

I have never had a single original idea in my entire life. Are you really seriously suggesting I can learn to do this?

Yes, I am.

Put your doubts aside. Send the voices on vacation. Make the symbols. Play honestly. and when you get your very first original vision, once you've recovered enough from the surprise and joy of it, send me a gift so I get to celebrate as well. ☺

Can you give an example how can I use the Genius Symbols to eliminate my personal blocks to abundance specifically?

There are many of different ways to use the symbols to work with something specific like "my personal blocks to abundance."

Here are just some ideas of the top of my head.

- Discover what blocks there are by going through the symbols one at a time and asking of each one, "Show me what blocks to abundance I have in the realms of (time, space, weather/emotion, aspects etc.)." That gives a good basic assessment and starts a process with awareness of what's wrong, and where, which is always a good step to starting to fix anything.
- You can go through them for ideas and insights how to overcome any blocks to abundance and achieve more abundance by picking up each one in turn, holding it to your heart and saying, "How can I use (space, time, people, light etc.) to (gain abundance/further abundance/overcome my blocks to abundance)?"
- You can play a Classic Game to discover and resolve a specific and/or majorly important block to abundance (that's my favourite, really!)
- You can certainly make a symbol sphere for charging charms to help dissolve blocks to abundance
- You can do meditations such as the blessings and gratitude meditation, in which you consider what blessings you already have in the (space, time, land, creativity etc.) department and show your gratitude, which often opens up the flow for MORE coming through
- You can do a specific "Wishes and Wants" exercise in which you take a symbol at a time and state what you actually want in terms of (space, time, trade, artefacts, house etc.) so that your energy mind can know what you mean by abundance in the first place and go to work to help manifest these things for you

- You can use all the symbols or just specific ones to create powerful, heartfelt affirmations by picking up a symbol at a time and saying, "My space is full of abundance/my time is full of abundance/etc." or any variation of an affirmation that makes sense to you.
- You can use the symbols to flash up memories relating to abundance, one for each symbol, to evolve limiting beliefs, values and feelings in the Events Psychology style with Project Sanctuary, EmoTrance or EFT.
- You can use the symbol pantheon to ask for the support of "The spirit of time/the spirit of dance/the spirit of trade etc." in your endeavours.
- You can pick out an individual symbol and carry it with you throughout the day, and take note of relevant insights relating to how you handle (time, space, gifts, people, spirits, trades, light etc.) which may need to be adjusted in order to achieve maximum wealth and abundance.

These are some ideas to get you going, I'm sure there is much, much more that can be done with the symbols. They are very versatile and combine well with other forms of change and self healing and invite deeply meditative/magical states where one starts to be guided in the right direction, and what one needs to do next, which is the best way to resolve or evolve any problem.

How can I introduce the Genius Symbols to my family/therapy clients/business clients without them thinking I'm weird?

This is a question I am asked often, and I have come to the conclusion that these days, people are much more open to such things as The Genius Symbols than they were 40 years ago when the New Age was in its infancy and beset with all manner of silly things that hurt the heads of logical and sensible people.

So first of all, don't be afraid. Simply bring out your (attractive) symbol set and place it somewhere where people can see it. Mostly, young, old, new age or technical minded alike, they will ask questions about it, are interested in the symbols, and will nod when you say that they are a simple kind of alphabet to talk to the energy mind which is the head of the energy body and was previously known as the sub- or unconscious mind.

As a first introduction, I don't talk beyond that and ask people to pick a symbol that they are drawn to, or simply one at random.

Then I ask them if they like to guess what that symbols means.

Most of the time, even young children end up in the right ballpark, and I will tell them what the symbol means in the context of The Genius Symbol game.

I will then explain how you "ask the symbols" by making a contract, and encourage them to put a question to the set, or let them try one of the simple warm up games, such as how to flash up a funny memory by looking at the symbol.

People engage very easily with the Genius Symbols; that was a part of the contract I made with my energy mind before we set off to create the Genius Symbols as they are today.

As long as you can stay relaxed and let people interact with the symbols freely, most people are fascinated by them and want to know more, and try something out for themselves – or in other words, they want to play with the symbols.

That's the first step and best result, and you can take it from there.

How can I use the Genius Symbols to generate ideas for a new product, for example in a staff meeting?

Make sure at the beginning of the meeting that you state the contract, the reason that you're all here, out aloud and write a reminder of the exact contract on a whiteboard, or on a piece of paper with large enough letters so that anyone who is present can see that.

Indeed you might then take some time to refine the contract, taking it from "we're just randomly brainstorming and hoping for the best" to "Give us an idea for a new product that will sell like hotcakes to our already existing customers, is quick and easy to implement, and make this company lots of money."

Now that is a good contract we can work with.

Then, simply put the Genius Symbols in the middle of the table and ask people to pick one each and give their idea for that new product.

If all the people present are painfully shy, tell them to write the idea down on their note pad so they can be collected and read out later on.

Encourage them to be quick, to jot down whatever came to mind quickly, then tell them to put the symbol back, and everyone picks another one.

You should do at least 5 – 7 symbols each to get a flow of ideas going, and a flow of writing. With five minutes for each symbol, seven symbols each takes 35 minutes, so you can spend the rest of the meeting going through the ideas you have generated and vote on the one you like the best if you want.

Now bear in mind, this is an example of **the first time ever** that these people have played with the symbols. You will already get some ideas, many more than you would have otherwise had, and that's first time out.

If the same people met again, all of this, from creating a better contract, to generating the ideas, to sorting them out at the end will become **exponentially faster** with practice and their output will produce better and **better quality ideas** with practice too.

So if you really want to generate ideas for your company or department, for your family which is a type of company too, for your school class, scout troop, healing circle, support group, political party or any meeting of people with a common goal, think of this as the path towards creating a real "genius session" and do it more than once only.

Just imagine the results you will get a year down the line, as your genius ideas creators become more practised and have had hard feedback from the implementation of the previous ideas to add to their experience. This is absolutely priceless, so get started, keep doing it, and learn to do this process of creativity and innovation well. With just a few more of us doing this, it can and will change the world.

I am fascinated by this and want to learn more. What can I do next?

I would first of all advise to **read this book more than once**. There is a lot of information contained in these pages that won't come alive for you until you have played a few games of your own, had your own first flash visions and gained some experience with how the Genius Symbols work.

I would like to add that the most learning is going to be achieved by playing the games. Play the games and allow yourself to become fascinated by your own mind and how it works. Pay attention, stay light, make a note of your experiences and keep a journal. That is what I call wisdom learning which will give you the best results of all.

For further reading, I recommend the original Project Sanctuary manual which contains hundreds of examples, ideas and tips for playing the game in space and time. If you are really serious about the game, there is the Project Sanctuary Masters course which contains special exercises to speed up and expand the evolution of your abilities.

We also have an English language correspondence course for more in-depth study of The Genius Symbols, leading to a Genius Symbols Reader certificate. You can find details on www.genius23.com as well as other news from and about the Symbol World.

Epilogue: More Genius, Please!

As I am concluding work on this second edition of The Genius Symbols, anno 2011, I am more aware of and amazed at the absence of real innovative, genius ideas in mainstream life than I've ever been.

Once you start playing with The Genius Symbols and gaining your own multiple inspirational visions, flashes, stories, insights and threshold shifts, you will join me in this.

Working in collaboration with your energy mind doesn't just give you the ability to create cohesive and logical stories in all these different modalities; it also imbues you with the ability to tell when something is not real.

People who have no imagination, no access to their own energy mind and lack the ability to stream visions have across the ages turned to plagiarism as the only way out for a conscious mind that doesn't know where the next, or any, good idea should be coming from.

Plagiarism is when you take someone else's good idea and pass it off as your own.

This happens everywhere and all the time.

Plagiarists think that they can steal a bit of this, and a bit of that, and cobble it together into a kind of Frankenstein's monster and it's new, or relevant, or a contribution of some kind.

It is not.

No matter how lovingly crafted or how carefully stitched together, it will always remain a Frankenstein's monster – a thing without a soul, a thing without energy that holds it together and makes it real, makes it more than the sum of its parts.

- **When we get used to dealing with real data streams, we also start to notice when these are absent.**

An interesting side effect I have noticed by people playing with the Genius Symbols is that they start to complain bitterly about crime shows on the TV, for example a movie that features a serial killer – but what they are doing and who they are does not tally, they could not have possibly be that person and do those things "in the real world". Someone took a bunch of real crimes, a few Freudian and pop psychology ideas, mashed them together, and created a Frankenstein's monster that has no reality, no depth, because it has no real vision holding it together.

You can see, hear, feel, sense, taste and experience this across the board – the absence of real original visions in art, in photography, in music, in advertising, in product creation.

Then, there is this embarrassing thing that the plagiarists do which we named "Sticking a tail on it and calling it a weasel!"

This can also be seen everywhere, putting a pink bow on an existing product and calling it an innovation, or even a new product when it clearly is no such thing, just the same old same old, dressed up a bit to make it look better or more than it actually is.

Look to politics for examples of that, not just to art, business and marketing...

The reason that the plagiarists do this is because they are operating without access to their own energy minds; and the reason that people are constantly fobbed off and fooled by these Frankenstein creations is because they don't have access to their energy minds either, and so have no way to stand up and say, "This is garbage!" although they know it somehow, sense the presence of this wrongness and it makes them feel vaguely uncomfortable, vaguely sad, empty, somewhat disappointed, even if they can't consciously explain why they're feeling that way.

I have personally found that having a bit of access to and support from my energy mind has always provided me with many, many solutions, ideas, new ideas, new things to try out, spotting things that others didn't seem to notice, and of course, an endless stream of original creativity.

It has driven me mad for decades that I could do these things, and other people would or could not.

For the first quarter of my life, I thought there was simply something fundamentally wrong with me and I accepted it as a given that I was doomed to be the one and only ideas man and the goto guy for any artistic or creative endeavours, wherever I happened to be.

Then I began to question this and as I spent more time researching and modelling what it was that I did, and how I did that, I also started to try out sharing some of the things I do with others.

And here I learned to my great surprise that the capacity for genius is global, it exists in all people who have even half a brain, but they were never encouraged to use it, or taught how to use it, and what they had been taught seemed custom made to stop people from accessing their own innate genius systems.

I also learned that in spite of all the counter-conditioning, in spite of all the brainwashing, the negative entrainments, the societal pressures, the mental malnourishment and the active attempts to kill off real visionary thinking in human beings, **they still all dream, they still all have memories, they still have thoughts, they still have secret fantasies and they all still have visions sometimes**, even if they didn't know what it was or didn't know what to do with that.

The systems are there and they will not be eradicated.

Thank GOD for that.

Our systems for real, expansive, fantastic and truly awesome human thought are real, everyone has them, and they can be awoken.

So I made it my business for the next quarter of a century to find out what we have to do to make that happen.

These genius systems we have are natural, and one of my original research contracts was to therefore find a way to make it as natural as possible to use, play with and activate these genius systems so we can learn more about them.

Project Sanctuary and discovering the true nature and language of the energy mind (or subconscious mind as it was known back then) was the major breakthrough in this quest.

From there, we learned that you can't treat human systems that are supposed to co-operate in a hierarchical way and that the conscious mind and the energy mind must be equal partners in the thinking game.

Here, we learned that playing games is better than dour study or endless chanting; we learned that visions are full modality, lucid experiences, and we learned about the extraordinarily interactive nature of the data flow.

We found endless surprises, and we found the threshold shifts, which gave us something to aim for, and something we could tell people as a reason for doing all these strange things with our minds in the first place – you want to get smarter, you want to heal, you need threshold shifts, evolutionary events that move your systems on to the next level of functioning.

Now Project Sanctuary in its pure form can keep you busy for a lifetime; and more than that, in playing in Sanctuary your get gifts along the way, EmoTrance being one of them, that take on a life of their own and this can detract from the original purpose of the research and enquiry – how to turn more people into real geniuses who can then go out and make stuff that is better than what we have right now.

I'll come back to that notion in a moment; here, we were playing in Sanctuary, having fantastic experiences - but there was a "but."

Unfortunately, you cannot get people who don't already have a notion that their mind is fascinating and that they may well have genius potential to play Project Sanctuary.

It is too far away from their every day experience; they can't see the relevancy of telling fairy tales for evolution; and they don't look to their own energy mind for providing them with outstanding solutions.

So there was a time when I was very frustrated with the inability of taking Project Sanctuary into the hard in a more effective way, and asked for some guidance on the topic, and so I was shown the first of the Genius Symbols one day.

It was a galaxy which stood for the entire material universe on that occasion, and the symbol is the spiral we have in the Genius Symbols today.

Thus, creating my Rosetta stones as a direct bridge between energy mind and unconscious mind came into being; and that changed the nature of the game, as it were.

Now, anyone can learn to play Project Sanctuary who wants to.

We tested the symbols with a wide variety of people, from all different economic strata and educational backgrounds, including some who could not read or write; very young children; teenagers; therapists; business people with no interest in anything esoteric or therapeutic whatsoever; and very importantly to me, with people from widely varying cultural backgrounds.

When I found that Australian Aborigines as well as German, Chinese, Egyptian, African and Brazilian people all responded to the symbols much in the same way, I knew I had what I wanted – something that works globally with humans across the board.

To me, this means that the Genius Symbols are structurally correct enough to do the job of making that all important bridge between the conscious mind and the energy mind.

Controlling the visions with the contracts was a significant aspect in the development of the process.

By taking out the fear and terror of uncontrollable "unconscious" materials being spewed out like the hordes of doom coming out of the gates of hell, we have restored sanity, peace, tranquillity to the process of contacting the energy mind and beginning to interact with its output.

That is the first step in breaching the divide; and with this first step established, everything else is easy and simply becomes a truly autodidactic process of personal learning and evolution for each and every person who starts to engage with their own energy mind.

To this day, I still call Project Sanctuary "The Greatest Game On Earth".

I think this is so because I have never found anything more fascinating that the human mind set free to be what it can be; and also, because all games on Earth, as anything else that people will do and make, always come from that realm and nowhere else.

Any other game by definition is nothing more than a by-product of The Greatest Game On Earth, as are all inventions, all innovation, all stories ever told in any modality, in any language, in any religion, in any science.

So you might say that by doing the best I can to increase the numbers of people quite practically who will go forth and inject brand new, genius ideas into their daily lives and their practices, I want to save the world and people from themselves.

And that is certainly true to a degree – but I'm also very selfish.

I yearn, and I really **yearn** with all my heart, for better, more logical, more beautiful, more joyful, more elegant **genius solutions to just about everything.**

I want sofas that are both comfortable and yet small enough to not take over entire rooms like the left over carcases of deceased dinosaurs.

I want traffic systems in my town that help drivers and business alike and are elegant genius solutions to the problems at hand.

I want shopping carts that don't break my back in loading and unloading.

I want to switch on my TV and be totally blown away by the plethora of fantastic new stories being told, and the news reports of science breakthroughs and genius conflict resolutions.

I want intelligent logical solutions at the genius level to the banking and commerce systems of the world; to age old questions of philosophy, religion and science; to health care; to human life full stop.

The list of what I want to see, touch, feel, taste, scent and sense before I die is veritably endless.

We need more people thinking at the genius level of systemic flow and integrative logic absolutely everywhere.

We need them as law makers, as politicians; as software designers; as business people; as mothers and fathers; as writers and artist; as surgeons and cooks; as furniture makers, space ship designers, road builders and bricklayers.

I absolutely believe that there isn't a problem on Earth that could not be either solved completely or at least evolved along on a path towards a solution by the application of more logic, more intelligence, and more creativity all aligned and working together as they should.

And you, my dear reader, can now be one of these new genius people who bring their genius solutions to their own special field of interest.

I challenge you – make a contribution!

It doesn't have to be "world peace overnight" or "the cure for cancer".

Give me an original story that excites me, find a cost cutting solution in your department that brings down my electricity bill, create a new form of customer service that will revolutionize my shopping experience in ASDA and make a million people's lives better by doing so.

Whatever your own fascinations are, whatever your fields of endeavour or skill, simply apply your new-found genius insights and ideas right there – and the world will become a better place as more and more genius wakes up and helps transform all our lives in every way imaginable.

Once you have created a few genius solutions, no matter how small or large they may be, and you have understood that you have the capacity to function at the genius level, as we all do, for the love of God, don't stop and sit down on your laurels.

Let's redefine the word genius to mean much more than just one good idea in a lifetime for which you got a Nobel prize.

Genius is streaming ideas all the time, learning how to stream these ideas at will and whatever the time or place you might find yourself in.

Don't let one single idea side track or derail you – no matter how good it was, how precious, know that there will always be more ideas and better ideas in that amazing, infinite stream of logical creativity that happens when both our minds get on the same page and become more than the sum of the parts.

So it is never about the idea – understand this is about you.

You are the hope for humanity.

You are, and I am, and every person who understands what I'm saying here and is willing to step up and take charge of their own minds, and in doing so, really does have the power to transform the experiences of other people's lives absolutely.

We – the human race – are badly in need of genius solutions.

We have the hardware given by the creative order which empowered us to create havoc on an epic scale, but also to learn of the error of our ways and evolve our solutions so we get out of humanity's eternal chaos and into some kind of Even Flow with the rest of the universe.

The Genius Symbols are a form of first generation software for the human mind, and they work.

Now it's over to you.

And the good news?

All you have to do is **start to play**.

Awaiting **YOUR** genius contributions,

Dr Silvia Hartmann

Creator, The Genius Symbols, January 1st, 2011

Further Information

Books & Manuals

Paperbacks/eBooks available from
www.DragonRising.com
and all good bookshops

Project Sanctuary – The Original Manual

The original Project Sanctuary manual by Dr S Hartmann contains a myriad of stories, ideas and in depth discussions of Project Sanctuary, plus a full & fascinating addendum of patterns and techniques that have come about as a result of many people using Project Sanctuary in their own way, all around the world.

Magic, Spells & Potions

Bringing magic out of the dark ages and into the light, this essential guide to modern energy magic by Dr Silvia Hartmann also contains a lot of additional information how to use The Genius Symbols in esoteric, metaphysical and paranormal contexts as a magic machine.

The flexibility and energy of the Genius Symbols can be used in many different ways in modern energy magic, from charging charms and imprinting water to creating extraordinary psychic readings and much more besides.

Oceans Of Energy – EmoTrance Volume 1

The 6th Sense of humans is feeling energy through the body – physical sensations that have no physical origin. Otherwise known as emotions, here is a whole new representation system that has been overlooked and completely misunderstood.

By putting energy into the equation, both energy work and human emotions become logical, make sense, but more than that – we can naturally learn to transform emotional energies to produce completely different feelings and sensations, naturally.

Oceans of Energy is the book that demystifies emotions, puts them in their rightful place and in doing so, unlocks a whole new universe filled with useful energy forms a person can use to change the experiences of their lives. Essential reading for modern human beings.

Events Psychology

People change, learn and evolve by experiencing events – threshold shifts that change the entire mind/body/energy system in a heartbeat. Conclusions consciously drawn from these events are the basis for all belief formation, and the beliefs will stay put until another event changes them again.

Events are pivotal to all human endeavour; in the remedial sense, trauma events, Guiding Star events and missing events need to be dealt with, but EvP shows us that if we want to learn, heal or evolve, we also need to create new events to take us to the next level. Highly Recommended.

Courses

The Genius Symbols Course

This course is designed by Dr Silvia Hartmann with delightful, surprising exercises to give you the practice and experience you need to make the extraordinary tools that are The Genius Symbols come to life.

Especially designed for the Distance Learning student and with full tutor support, this is a great way to ensure that you do the practice you know you need to really unlock your potential for formulating powerful contracts, receiving and streaming visions, and taking the information through to practical action as well. For details, please visit:

www.Genius23.com

The Project Sanctuary Masters Course

Study Project Sanctuary in-depth with the Project Sanctuary Master's course. A true journey of personal transformation, you are working with your own threshold shifts throughout. This course contains many extraordinary exercises, ideas and challenging patterns, devised for those who really want to stretch their minds by Dr Silvia Hartmann.

For details and to enrol, please visit:

www.Sidereus.org

Audio Energy Hypnosis Programs

Project Sanctuary - The Far Journeys

The Far Journeys take the traveller way, way outside the realms of ordinary awareness, and sometimes the journeys are so far outside that an interim "staging post" is need to transfer further out. These energy hypnosis journeys are a device to help train the conscious mind to keep aware, keep lucidity and widen its abilities to manage highly complex and intensely information rich data streams that are not encountered in the hard. Also includes the bonus "Earth Rise" visualisation training CD.

The Appollonius Quartet

Exquisite PS derived program to enhance and restore psychic abilities and the psychic circuitry. Four journeys that together make more than the sum of their parts to reach and work with the psychic circuitry, created by Dr Silvia Hartmann.

The HypnoDreams Trilogy

The acclaimed HypnoDreams series contains journeys to different loci – shared universal habitats to which people have travelled through the ages. The HypnoDreams series very literally "expands the boundaries of the mind" and allows especially Project Sanctuary users to have fantastic experiences in transformation, time, space and the multifold dimensions.

Project Sanctuary Based Books

The Enchanted World

The Enchanted World is a brilliant introduction to the worlds of energy, and a fascinating journey through the presuppositions of Dr Silvia Hartmann's universe. For Project Sanctuary players, there are many useful ideas, techniques and pathways to be found here; this is also a good first introduction to EmoTrance, which comes in very handy in many different situations. The Enchanted World can still be downloaded for free from http://starfields.org - and there is also a German language version called Zauberwelt available and a Spanish version, Mundo Encantado.

Paperback available from
www.DragonRising.com
and all good bookshops

The Golden Horse

The Golden Horse contains 15 fascinating Project Sanctuary stories, linked together by the central idea of the storytellers "who bind the Universe". This is an excellent example of using Project Sanctuary to generate stories that produce actual neurological change in the reader; as well as being an outstanding example how language can be used to transmit data in a hypnotic and elegant way. For a student of Project Sanctuary, the stories themselves and also the connections between the stories, offer a treasure chest of stimulation, ideas and a springboard for their own explorations.

Paperback/eBook available from
www.DragonRising.com
and all good bookshops

The Soul Pilots, 1

A "must read" for all Project Sanctuary players. Filled with the most exquisite, stimulating, moving visions by 9 Project Sanctuary Masters, this book has a long lasting effect on the reader, inspiring them to undertake their own Soul Piloting journeys and transform their ideas of self, others, life, death, and the immortal soul.

Paperback/eBook available from
www.DragonRising.com
and all good bookshops

The Soul Pilots, 2: Evolutions

Hot in the heels of the first and original Soul Pilots book comes "Soul Pilots: Evolution" which features BRAND NEW soul-piloting stories. Also included are full instructions for writing your own.

Paperback/eBook available from
www.DragonRising.com
and all good bookshops

Project Sanctuary Visionary Fiction by StarFields

The Magician contains many examples of linking up planes, habitats and events in order to achieve an aim – have the player metamorphose from an ordinary person into a true magician. Rich in detail and immensely rich in multi-level information, this story, which was created by tuning into the vision once every night for 28 days, demonstrates many principles of Sanctuary work, as well as being a true inspiration for PS players.

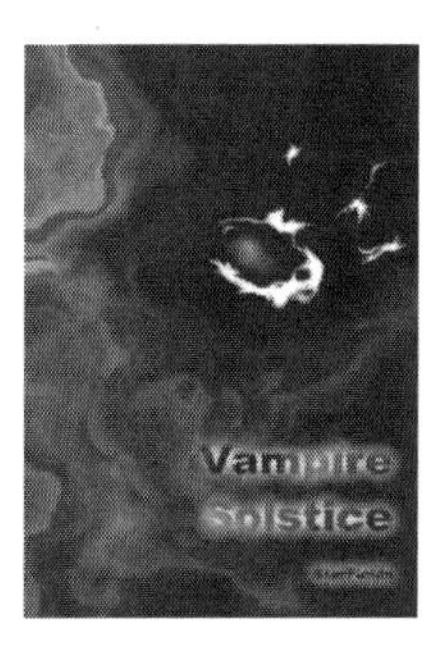

Vampire Solstice Absolutely fascinating, amazing energies, scenarios, events and exchanges in energy, this is a classic Project Sanctuary novel that changes the way we think about many things but especially in this case about love, evolution and preciousness. An outstanding example of Project Sanctuary fiction at its best.

In Serein The In Serein Trilogy by Starfields is an amazing book, an amazing story, a Project Sanctuary meta story like no other.

High energy, high magic and the topics are love and power, absolution, good and evil.

Once read, never forgotten.

Paperback/eBook available from
www.DragonRising.com
and all good bookshops

SpaceNode Websites: A Genius Symbols Vision

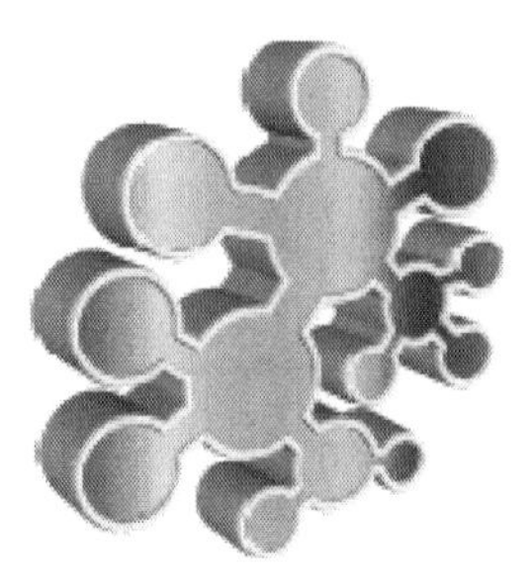

From a session utilising "The Genius Symbols" to generate business ideas, the concept behind SpaceNode Websites was born.

Now in use by beginners and experts alike, SpaceNode offers a revolutionary approach to giving people their own websites which are great at attracting visitors from search engines and social networks.

Some of the highlights of owning a SpaceNode include...

- Suitable for beginners and experts to create their own websites for personal and business use
- Take total control of your website through the SpaceNode easy-to-use web interface
- Choose your site theme to change how your site looks
- Create unlimited blogs
- Create unlimited pages and folders online
- Create unlimited contact forms – never put your real email online again
- Comes complete with advanced site-search technology courtesy of the SpaceNode Spider
- Have your website found and indexed quickly by search engines using unique SpaceNode technology
- Integrate your website with Facebook, Twitter and other websites
- Store your files, downloads and images online to attract people to your site
- Choose your own website name and create your own professional *you@you.com* email addresses
- Create unlimited SpaceNode websites and control them all through the easy-to-use SpaceNode admin panel

Internet Resources

www.Genius23.com – Genius unleashed with the Genius Symbols. News, articles and reports from the symbol world.

www.ProjectSanctuary.com – All things Project Sanctuary – news, stories, visions, latest developments and more.

www.DragonRising.com – The home of Project Sanctuary and all its children in traditional and e-publishing.

www.Sidereus.org – Online certification programs for Genius Symbol Readers, EmoTrance Energy Work and Project Sanctuary Players and Masters, certified through The Sidereus Foundation.

www.StarFields.org – Online catalogue of Dr Hartmann's available research, writings and training programs.

www.SilviaHartmann.com – Dr Hartmann's home pages which include sections on Project Sanctuary, creativity, art, EmoTrance and more.

www.HypnoDreams.org – Home of Dr Hartmann's energy hypnosis products, guided meditations, advanced energy hypnosis programs and the original HypnoDreams trilogy.

www.1-art.eu – Dr Hartman's art, design, sculpture and illustrations site with information on Energy Art, Art Solutions, exhibitions, news and the Art network.

www.1-poem.com – Dr Hartmann's poetry site, pecialising in energy mind derived poetry and poems.

www.SoulPilots.com – The Soul Pilots headquarters on the world wide web.

www.EmoTrance.com – Home of the most advanced and most logical energy modality in the world today. Events, courses, practitioners, trainers, news, free downloads, forums and international EmoTrance community.

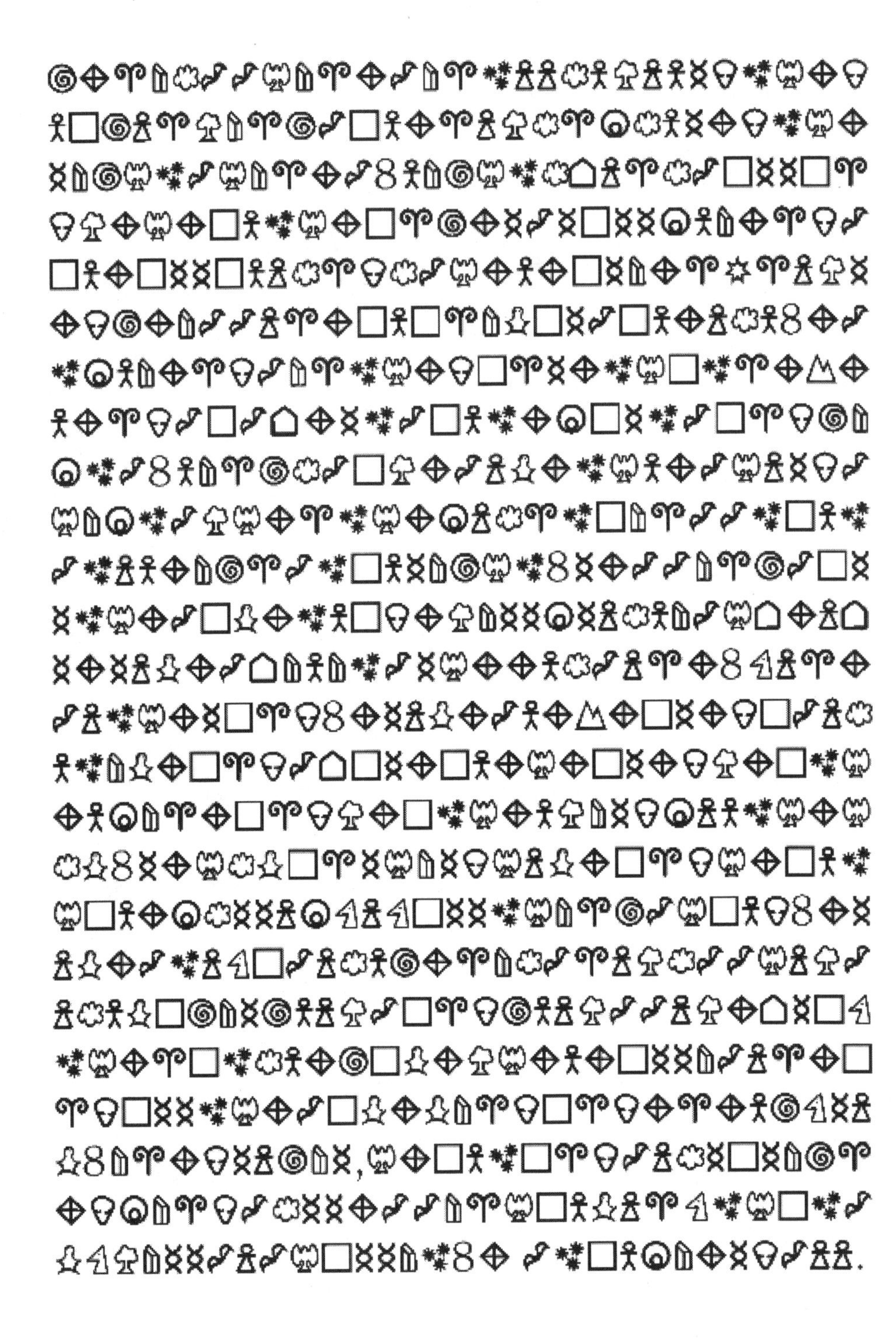